# NHL PROSPECTS 2011 DRAFT

© 2010 by The Hockey Press
All rights reserved.

ISBN  0986538612

EAN-13  9780986538612.

Printed in the USA

# Photo Credits

Tyler Wotherspoon, Ty Rattie -Soobum Im/Portland Winterhawks

Tyler Hansen, Colin Smith - Tricia Mercuri.

Dylan lynch Edmonton Oil kings

David Connell QMJHL Images

Mark McNeil - Thomas Porter Photographs

Seth Ambroz -USHL Images

CHL Images - Aaron Bell & Terry Wilson

WHL.ca

OntariohockeyLeague.com

lhjmq.qc.ca

Shane McColgan - Andrew Echevarria

Reece Scarlett, Adam Lowry - scbroncos.com

Marc Line - QMJHL Photos

Timothy Kane Photography

Dave Arnold Sports Photography

# Table of Contents

| | | | |
|---|---|---|---|
| 3. | Ryan Murphy | 98. | Matt Puempel |
| 8. | Daniel Catenacci | 105. | Jordan Binnington |
| 12. | Garrett Meurs | 109. | Nathan Beaulieu |
| 16. | Zach Bell | 113. | Nick Shore |
| 21. | Colin Smith | 117. | Cameron Brace |
| 25. | Jesse Forsberg | 122. | Jonathan Huberdeau |
| 29. | Shane McColgan | 128. | Sean Couturier |
| 36. | Tyler Wotherspoon | 133. | Brandon Saad |
| 42. | Ty Rattie | 137. | Patrick Koudys |
| 47. | Graeme Craig | 142. | Scott Mayfield |
| 52. | Mitch Topping | 147. | Klarc Wilson |
| 60. | Tyler Biggs | 152. | Adam Lowry |
| 66. | Alan Quine | 158. | Seth Ambroz |
| 71. | Tyler Hansen | 162. | Mark McNeill |
| 77. | Kale Kessy | 166. | Travis Ewanyk |
| 82. | Zack Hall | 170. | Franky Palazzese |
| 87. | Tomas Jurco | 174. | Ryan Nugent-Hopkins |
| 91. | Michael St. Croix | 179. | Reece Scarlett |

# Three Horse Race?

They say good things come in threes. That can certainly be said about the race for top overall player in the 2011 NHL Entry Draft. Three players in particular are vying for No. 1 pick honors in Sean Couturier, Adam Larsson and Ryan Nugent-Hopkins. Each has exceptional skills, but only one will hear his name called as the first selection. So it begs the question: how will one of the National Hockey League's struggling franchises choose between the trio? It comes down to that team's core drafting beliefs. Do you take the best player available or draft by positional need?

There is not much separating the three players at this stage in the process. With the various league's seasons underway, much will be decided as the year rolls along. But one thing is for sure. Each has a solid claim to be the No. 1 pick.

Couturier is a dominant skilled forward for the Drummondville Voltigeurs of the Quebec Major Junior Hockey League. He tied

for the league lead in scoring last season with 41 goals and 55 assists for a whopping 96 points in just 68 games. With his 6-foot-3, 185-pound frame, he is great down low and more than willing to go to the hard areas to score. Couturier protects the puck very well with his long reach. Known as more of a finisher, he is also very adept as a passer and possesses superior vision. Scouts also like how mature Couturier's defensive game has become. He is one of the more talented two-way players in recent years. If he can improve his first few skating strides, Couturier could prove to be a lethal offensive weapon at the NHL level.

The latest big name in the long line of top-notch Swedish defensemen is Adam Larsson. At almost 6-foot-3 and 200 pounds, Larsson has ideal size for a blueliner. To add to his superior stature, Larsson is a fantastic skater with good quickness and top speed. He has already played professionally at Sweden's top level. Two years of professional hockey will be awfully appealing to an NHL franchise looking for a player to make an immediate impact. Larsson is very poised for a young player and makes a great breakout pass. With his booming shot and solid vision, Larsson netted 4 goals and 13 assists in 49 games for Skelleftea HC of the Swedish Elite League last season. While his offensive skills are impressive, Larsson is no slouch in his own zone. He uses his big frame to push opponents off the puck and has a good stick-check as well. Larsson's combination of size, skill, smarts and physicality will make him hard to pass on for the team with the first pick this June.

While Couturier and Larsson were absent from the NHL's Research and Development Camp, Nugent-Hopkins, a shifty center for the Red Deer Rebels of the Western Hockey League, had a chance to grab the spotlight. That is not to say he has come out of the blue as he was the top selection in the WHL Bantam Draft in 2008. HP has been very fond of Nugent-Hopkins for a long time. He is rather slight at 6-feet and 160 pounds but has elite offensive skills. He is a very good skater with great quickness. Nugent-Hopkins has a laser for a shot and is very accurate. Like all great players, he has unbelievable hockey-sense and vision. In his first full WHL season, Nugent-Hopkins popped in 24 goals and 41 assists in 2009-10. He won Rookie of the Year honors for his exceptional play. If that was not enough to open some eyes, he scored the game-winner in the championship game of the Ivan Hlinka Memorial Tournament to beat the United States in August. Once he adds some muscle to his slim frame, Nugent-Hopkins could be the best pick of the draft.

# The Interviews

# Ryan Murphy
## Defense - Kitchener Rangers

Ryan Murphy of the Kitchener Rangers was the 3rd overall selection in the 2009 OHL Priority selection. Prior to becoming a Kitchener Ranger, Murphy played for a very strong York Simcoe Express team which featured multiple OHL draft picks including the 1st overall selection, Daniel Catenacci.

The Aurora Ontario native brings fantastic offensive abilities to his game. Murphy popped in 6 goals and added an outstanding 33 assists in his rookie season as a Ranger. Ryan hopes to improve on those numbers as he heads into his NHL Draft season.

## The Interview:

HP: How did your first season in Kitchener go?

RM: It was a pretty good season. I learned a lot, mostly on the defensive side. I thought as a team we did really well, but hopefully next year we can do even better.

HP: It seems you learned to rush the puck while playing with York Simcoe. Was there a difference between the coaching there and in Kitchener?

RM: Yeah, he [Catenacci] always said to me it was all about the offense; defense is something you will learn later but you need to learn the offense while you still can. So, whenever I could he told me to go with the puck.

HP: Was it tough to adjust to a less puck-rushing role and more into a defensive system?

RM: It wasn't too bad. Steve Spott is a really good coach and he taught me a lot of defense. I don't know if any other team could teach me like he did. But, he still lets me do my thing too, so I like it.

HP: Speaking of teaching defense, you aren't the biggest guy in the world and probably aren't knocking around older and bigger players. How much has his teaching helped you still be an effective defenseman despite not being as big?

RM: He knows I'm not the biggest guy. I'm going to be working on that in the summers to come. But, I like to stick check a lot, good body positioning, so I can rub guys off and just go for the puck and do it that way.

HP: What was the toughest adjustment playing in the OHL this season?

RM: I think just getting to know my team. I was playing with older guys now and I needed to know my role, I was a rookie; I couldn't be chirping other guys. Of course there is the opponents being bigger and stronger but as the year went on I got used to that. So, overall just getting used to playing with the bigger guys.

HP: Did any defensemen on Kitchener help you adjust this past season?

RM: Yeah, I'd say Dan Kelly and John Moore taught me a lot; they kind of took me under their wing a bit. Without them I don't know if I could have done as well.

HP: Over the course of the year, did you feel yourself progressively improving and becoming more confident?

RM: At the beginning of the year I think I was playing decent because I was just so focused on not making mistakes in the defensive zone. But, as the year went on I realized my spot on the team is not the major defensive role, even though it may become that. I needed to produce some points, get a little more free-wheeling to create some offense.

HP: There is a real dynamic element to your game in terms of rushing the puck from the defensive end. What other strengths do you think you have?

RM: Yeah, I really like to rush the puck, but I learned this year it is better to move the puck then get up into the play. Otherwise, I think I'm a good skater and have good vision.

HP: What about some improvements you want to make?

RM: I have a lot to improve on for next year. I want to do as a good as I can so I need to get better in the defensive zone. I want to be a plus next year and I need to get a lot bigger and stronger if I want make it to the next level someday.

HP: In terms of the next level, have you been thinking about the 2011 draft at all or are you just focusing on success with Kitchener?

RM: Individual success is good, but I'd like to see the team go to the Memorial Cup here. That would be great to win a championship in the OHL especially in Kitchener with such a great group of guys.

HP: You guys had a really good run in the playoffs this year. What was that experience like?

RM: It was unbelievable .We had a really young team, only 6 guys without playoff experience. It was all about getting some experience and we got 20 games, brought Windsor to seven, beat London in seven, and played some pretty good hockey. I think at the end of the day we were happy with ourselves.

HP: We spoke with Jeff Skinner over the season who expressed a desire to lead the team into the playoffs. As a younger player, how effective was he in that sense?

RM: Yeah, Jeff was the leader on and off the ice. Everyone respected him in the room, and when it came down to it we knew he would always get that goal to win the game.

HP: Do you foresee yourself taking on a leadership role with the team next season?

RM: I want to take on a leadership role. It doesn't matter if I get a letter on my jersey, but I want to help the younger rookies, because I know how it feels. But, yeah, I want to be a voice in the dressing room and get the guys going.

HP: Are there any defenseman either in the CHL or NHL that you like to watch play in terms of learning the position.
RM: I love to watch Alex Pietrangelo. He went to my school and my brother is pretty good friends with him and I think he is just an awesome defenseman. In the NHL, I love to watch Dan Boyle [San Jose Sharks] play. He is a great player

HP: What has been your most memorable moment in your hockey career so far?

RM: I would say Game Three in Windsor against Windsor and one of my buddies, Gabriel Landeskog scored the winner.

# Daniel Catenacci
## Center -Soo Greyhounds

The Soo Greyhounds made Daniel Catenacci the 1st overall pick in the 2009 OHL Priority selection. Catenacci played for his father who coached the York Simcoe Express in Daniel's draft season.

Catenacci had a successful rookie season with the Greyhounds as he scored 10 goals and added 20 assists. Daniel also scored in the playoffs in a series versus the Plymouth Whalers. The 5'10 " 180 pound speedy forward heads into his draft season on a Soo team which will now be two years removed from being dead last overall. Daniel should have a good returning cast this season with the Greyhounds.

# The Interview:

HP: How did it feel to be drafted #1 overall in the OHL draft?
DC: Being drafted was a huge honor and being on a list of guys such as Stamkos and Tavares was a dream come true.

HP: You spent much of your younger years playing with Ryan Murphy and now you guys are both high draft prospects on opposing teams. Has that been a fun experience?

DC: Yeah, Murph and I've been great friends all our lives. In the offseason we hang out almost every day so it's fun to play against each other and also hope to get drafted at the same time.

HP: How would you say your first year in the OHL went?

DC: It was pretty good. It was a lot of fun. It was a learning lesson for sure, but it taught me a lot and I think next year will be a lot better. I can take what I learned last year and apply it to next year.

HP: In terms of learning experiences, what are some of the lessons you got this season?

DC: I think my D-zone coverage got a lot better over the year. Other little things like having less time, being quicker with the puck, shooting a lot more because if you don't shoot then the puck isn't going in the net. I think in midget you get away with handling the puck a little more, but in the OHL you got to shoot to score goals.

HP: If you were a scout, what would you say were your biggest strengths?
DC: I would have to say my skating and my competitiveness for sure.

HP: Is it tough to control your competitiveness to make sure you are always in control?

DC: Yeah, when I have a bad shift sometimes I get down on myself, but I've learned more that when something doesn't go your way you just got to go out there and fix it your next shift instead of letting it snowball on you.

HP: What about if you were a scout and were looking at what you need to improve on?

DC: My overall speed and strength I think. This year I also got caught stick-handling too much and holding on to the puck too long. I'm working on shooting the puck more; quick release and just getting pucks on net.

HP: Have you had any nerves regarding the 2011 draft or is too early?

DC: Yeah, I think it's really far away. It will be pretty exciting to know it's my draft year, but it's not something I'm thinking about all year. My team has got to come first, so I'll keep it in the back of my mind.

HP: In terms of next year, what are some of your goals for the Soo Greyhounds?

DC: Well, two years ago we were the last placed team and I think this year we did a great job bouncing back from that. I think next year, we and the coaches really want to be a contender and one of the better teams in the league.

HP: Now that you will be a second year player, do you want to take more of a leadership role?

DC: Yeah, I try to lead with my competitiveness and my work ethic and next year if I do the same thing I will be in a good spot.

HP: Who have been some of the tougher defensemen you have had to go against this season?

DC: Playing against Pietrangelo from Barrie was really tough. He spent four years in the league, was a top five NHL Pick, and is big. I didn't get around him too many times. Guys like him and Dan Kelley off of Kitchener; just some of the more defensive and bigger guys.

HP: Are there any forwards in the OHL you have been able to learn from while playing?

DC: Playing against Tyler Seguin and Taylor Hall all year, I was in the same division as them and saw them quite a few times this year. While I was on the bench I was watching them and trying to understand what brings them success.

HP: What about a player you like to watch in the NHL?

DC: Yeah, I stick with Sidney Crosby. This year I tried to watch every game he played and know what he does out there.

HP: Do you have any individual goals for next season?
DC: Yeah, I've always thought of myself as a complete player and I want to continue working on all aspects of the game. I don't really have a statistical goal or bar I want to set, I just want to keep working on my game and helping the team.

HP: Now to finish up with one of the crazy NHL combine type of questions. If you were a part of a salad what part would you be?

DC: I'm not sure, but I guess I would be the dressing. A salad doesn't taste good without dressing.

# Garrett Meurs
## Center - Plymouth Whalers

Garrett Meurs is a 5'11 175 pound Centerman who hails from Ripley, Ontario. Meurs was the Whalers 1st round draft pick and was selected 13th overall in the 2009 OHL Draft.

Meurs built on a fantastic Minor Midget season with his Huron-Perth Lakers. Garrett had scored 52 goals with 43 assists for 95 points in 67 games with Huron Perth. This season with the Whalers he posted impressive numbers for a rookie with 16 goals and 18 assists. Meurs was also a +4 and had 22 penalty minutes in 62 games. Garrett also chipped in with 3 points in 9 playoff games.

# The Interview:

HP: How did your first season in the OHL go?

GM: My first season I got off to a good start by scoring in my second game, but it got necessary to slow things down, to take everything in and play simple.

HP: Was it a tough adjustment period?

GM: Yeah it took a while to get used to, but my teammates really helped me out with that teaching me the little things on and off the ice that you need to do to be successful.

HP: What are some examples of the little things you learned?

GM: Yeah, for example after practice going to the weight room to get a workout in and keep your muscles in good shape. On the ice, making sure you take advantage and work hard at every practice.

HP: What was it like playing and spending a season with an elite player like Tyler Seguin?

GM: I learned a lot by watching him. He worked so hard on and off the ice all the time. He is always doing something to make his game better. It pretty much showed me how he got to where he is right now.

HP: If you were scouting yourself what would you say some of your strengths are?

GM: Some of my strengths are definitely my speed, and how I try to compete every second on the ice and do the little things correctly.

HP: Where would you say most of your production comes from on the ice?

GM: Most of my production would come from going to the net, putting in the rebounds and those types of goals; hard work goals.

HP: What are some of the things you are trying to improve on for next year?

GM: I'm trying to improve on making sure I always know where my point man is, and playing on the wing. I'm trying to improve my defensive game a bit. Also I need to get stronger.

HP: What are some of the defensive improvements you are talking about?

GM: I got to work on where my man is. I seem to lose him too much for my liking, so I need to make sure I keep my head up on that.

HP: Are there any players in the OHL or NHL you like to watch play or think you can model your game after a bit?

GM: Well one guy on my team is AJ Jenks. He was our captain this year and I just love the way he plays. He is always competing and he is strong with a good shot. He also is always looking out for his teammates. He teaches the little things which is good for the rookies. In the NHL I love to watch Sidney Crosby. The way he plays the game is unbelievable and is a lot of fun to watch.

HP: What about any defenseman that have been particularly tough to play against?

GM: Ryan Ellis. Definitely playing against him. I had to play him eight times this season and you never knew what to expect. He could always catch you off guard.

HP: So, what are your goals for next season?

GM: My goal next year is just to improve on next year. I want to get better at everything on the ice, and that means improving on everything I did this season.

HP: Well, the draft is sort of just around the corner for you at this point. Any nerves about that?

GM: I haven't really thought about that yet. I'm starting to get there knowing that it is just a season away, but not thinking too much about it yet.

# Zach Bell
## Defense - Brampton Battalion

Zach Bell is another one of those players with 'NHL Bloodlines'. His birth father is former NHL'er Bruce Bell, who was selected by the Quebec Nordiques in the 3rd round in 1983. Bruce Bell played for Quebec, St. Louis, New York Rangers and the Edmonton Oilers for 1 game. Bell was a fourth round pick by the Battalion and played in 46 games as a rookie.

The 6'2 215 pound defenseman will enter the season with some veteran Brampton defenseman departed to the pro ranks. Bell will be on NHL scouts radar right off the hop next season given his blend of size, talent and toughness. Bell dropped the gloves in his rookie season with Stefan Della Rovere. That alone sums up the toughness.

# The Interview:

HP: How was your first year in the OHL with Brampton?

ZB: It was a pretty good year. I signed as a fourth rounder, played 46 games. We had a great D core and I played as much as I could; learned from guys like Matt Clark and Ken Peroff, the real defensive guys. I was able to figure out my role as a tough defenseman, who was real gritty, and good in the corners; makes the good first pass. In the end, it was great to learn my role and it makes me excited to grow off of it next year.

HP: Was adjusting to a new role a tough challenge?

ZB: Yeah, I'd say so. In my minor midget year, I played in every situation and got a lot of ice time. In Brampton, I started working on my pivots, and my skating. I realized I'm not going to score 40 goals in the "O", I do have some offensive skills, but for now anyway, I realized that I was going to be a shut down guy.

HP: Would you say once you found your role that the adjustment became much easier?

ZB: Yeah, I kind of figured out the flow of the game 20 games in or so. It's so much different then minor midget; so much faster. Everybody is a step ahead and knows where they are going with the puck. 20 or 30 games in I just kind of found out that I could really trust the guys on the team and I could just play my own game.

HP: What would you say are some of your strengths on the ice?

ZB: I'm a very physical player and for right now I'd say I'm a stay at home defenseman. Honestly, I'd like to play like Dion Phaneuf. If the option is there to join in the rush I want to, but I really want to focus on winning my battles, making a good first pass.

HP: So, what do you think you need to work on?

ZB: My forwards to backwards, transition stuff; skating around with my head up. I want to work on my offense a bit. I know my defense is pretty good, it can always improve, but I'd like to get better in the offensive end. I only had five points in 46 games, so I really want to round out my game in that way.

HP: You mention only getting 5 points last season but you had quite a few points in minor hockey. Is it hard to watch the older players get all the powerplay time?

ZB: Well any player would want to be out there (getting powerplay ice) of course, but at the same time I know that I'm a rookie and that players like Clark have earned their ice time, so it's easy to understand why the vets are on the PP. I think I'll get a chance on the PP at some point and I'll try to make the best of it when I do.

HP: How inspirational is it to see a guy like Dylan McIlrath who went from a low point, tough defenseman in his first season to a likely first round selection after his second season?

ZB: Yeah, for sure. I like to see guys like that and it inspires me to try and improve just as much. It is important for me to get drafted in 2011 as I really want to keep playing, obviously.

HP: Have you been thinking much about the draft?

ZB: I don't think it's hit me quite yet, the idea of being an NHL prospect. I'm more nervous about making sure I always make the right play, but I'm also just really excited for this year in Brampton.

HP: What would you say was the biggest difference you discovered this year between minor midget and the OHL?

ZB: Besides game speed stuff, I'd say being in the locker room as a rookie. It's so different; it's much more of a business like atmosphere. You can't be what you were in minor hockey; you aren't a top dog any more. I came in as a seventh D and now it's about showing them I'm here to work for however long they want me.

HP: Is it almost like you went from playing in a kid's league to an adult league?

ZB: Yeah, I'd say I walked in the first day still a kid. But, you see all these guys playing for pro contracts or to get drafted, and it makes you grow up quickly.

HP: So, what are some goals for next season?

ZB: I want to have a good plus/minus, fight some tough guys, score some goals, and have good body language. I just want to do everything well.

HP: Who are some NHL or OHL defensemen you like to watch play?

ZB: I like the Dion Phaneuf/Sheldon Souray's in the NHL. In the OHL, I like guys like Matt Clark, Cameron Guance; just the defensive guys that play real tough and make good passes.

HP: What are you working on this offseason?

ZB: Well, I'm doing power skating with Dawn Braid (former Toronto Maple Leafs skating instructor) a couple times a week to work on some technical stuff. I'm not slow out there, but I'm not exactly pretty either so I'd like to work on smoothing it out. In terms of getting bigger and stronger, putting on weight has never been an issue for me. I was 210/215 (pounds) all year last year. I just want to lean out and make sure I'm all muscle.

HP: You mention Dawn Braid working on your technical skating. A couple of our scouts have noted that you are actually a very fast skater. Has she helped improve your speed along with the technical side or do they go hand in hand?

ZB: This is the second year I have worked with her and she has really helped me. I think I have always surprised people with my speed, especially since I'm a pretty big guy. She has helped my speed get even better though, especially my first few steps. She has really helped with my edges, my stride, power and my hips as well.

HP: Zach, your birth father is former NHL player, Bruce Bell. It seems a lot of hockey people talk about NHL bloodlines more and more these days. What about this bloodlines stuff?

ZB: If I have been blessed with some natural ability because of him than that's a good thing I guess. He and my natural mother have not been a part of my life. I'll do more with my Uncle tomorrow (a Saturday) than I did with Bruce my whole life. My Aunt and Uncle are my legal parents now. They have been awesome to me and they have really helped me mature. I know I'm a better person and a better player since they took me in. I owe them so much for what they have done for me.

HP: Ok, time for one of those crazy NHL combine team interview type questions. Don't worry, we will only give you one of these. Here goes: You and your teammates are on a road trip and need to take taxis to get back to your hotel and beat curfew. Unfortunately you are only able to track down one cab and it can only hold four players max. You are the player with the money to pay the cab. What do you do?

ZB: (Laughs) Well, if I was the player with all the cab fare I'd probably stay with the team and keep sending the cab back and forth with 4 players per trip until we all made it back to the hotel. How long do we have until curfew? I would have left earlier from wherever we were!

# Colin Smith
## Forward - Kamloops Blazers

Colin Smith was selected as the Kamloops Blazers first round (7th overall pick) in the 2008 WHL Bantam Draft. Smith has come off an impressive season with the Edmonton CAC Canadians the previous year, totaling up 36 goals and 70 assists in 33 games.

Colin debuted as a rookie 16-year old in 2008, and made a solid impression with 4 points in only 8 games. He continued to register 21 points in 48 games the following season, despite battling a broken hand injury. A healthy Smith is going to improve his stock heading into his NHL Draft year.

# The Interview:

HP: You're from Edmonton so obviously hockey is popular there, but what do you think motivated you to start playing the game?

CS: I just started playing because my brother played and that's pretty much how I got started, my brother's three years older than me

HP: Any thoughts on your season?

CP: Well I broke my hand and was out the first ten weeks, so that was tough. Then I started pretty good, my season began going pretty well, then I kind of hit a drought time and then took it up to playoffs. When you're at a low point like that you have to figure yourself out and I really kind of cut the focus on my game, and turn it around.

HP: You had some pretty good points but your plus minus was at a negative eighteen,. What do you think you can improve for next season to get a better plus minus?

CS: Definitely the defensive side [of my game]. Some games I thought I played well, but I'd be minus two or something like that. My coach really stressed it and I actually got better near the end. And I think was even lower than [minus 18], but I brought it back up. I think it's just the fact that if I play defense first, offensive will come and that's good, so I just have to keep doing that.

HP: Who do you usually play with? How do you think they add to your game?

CS: I played with [Brendan Ranford] when I was in Bantam, so we have some good chemistry, so I played with him. I also played with [Dylan Willick] a lot, and then I played with [Chase

Schaber] a bit at the end. Definitely with Ranford, I think we play well together and make some plays.

HP: You're not a very big guy, how do you deal with physical play, with guys getting on you, do you have linemates that look out for you? Or are you not afraid to get into the play? How do you deal with big guys on you?

CS: I've been a small guy all my life, so I've just played like this all my life. But if you're scared, you're not going to be able to do anything, you just have to approach it. If there's anyone you against, show them your stuff, and if you get hit – you get hit. You're going to make it a lot harder for them to hit you if you're creating plays, dishing, and make moves and stuff like that. You have to make yourself hard to hit; keeping your feet moving and being big.

HP: How has the Blazers organization helped you develop your game?

CS: In everything, you're on the ice all the time, and the coaches have experience, as well as the other players and the older guys. You're in an environment where you can pretty much improve in every part of the game.

HP: So, what sorts of things do you want to improve on?

CS: Well, my size; getting bigger and stronger and then I'd have to say my shot too.

HP: Do you have any goals to go along with those?

CS: Not really, I'm just going to hope to just go play my game, try to help the team win, if the team succeeds, then individual success will come for everybody

HP: Who are some of the hardest defensemen to go against one on one in the WHL?

CS: I'll say Jared Cowen from Spokane

HP: Do you have any advice for Bantam or Midget players with big dreams out there?

CS: Just to always learn from your game. There's always going to be that guy who's ahead of you, who's better at something than you, but never be satisfied with where you're at and just keep trying to get better and better, if you want to get into the WHL, you can.

HP: As you know, in the NHL Combines, there are really odd questions that really help scouts learn more about you, so here's one just for practice; How many golf balls do you think you can fit in a school bus?

CS: A school bus? (laughs) fifty-thousand?

# Jesse Forsberg
## Defense - Prince George Cougars

Jesse Forsberg was a 1st round pick by the Cougars in the 2008 WHL Bantam Draft. He was the 11th overall pick that draft. Forsberg played his first Western Hockey League game for the Cougars in January of 2009 against the Tri-City Americans. Jesse Played for Team West at the 2010 World Under-17 Challenge in Timmins, Ontario.

Forsberg is a tough, gritty defenseman with good offensive instincs. He should get an increase in icetime this coming season and have full opportunity to showcase himself to NHL scouts in his draft year.

## The Interview:

HP: How did your first season with Prince George go?

JF: Well, it was tough obviously losing a lot. But, personally, I got to play in all positions and in many roles that generally first year players don't get to. So, in that sense it was a good year for me.

HP: Would you say that being thrust into such a big role so early made you adjust quicker?

JF: Yeah, for sure. I started here kind of intimidated as a 16 year old, thinking I'd just fill in. But, as soon as the season started I got put into a big role so I had to react quick and perform, which helped me grow a bit.

HP: What would you say was the toughest thing about joining the WHL this season?

JF: The toughest thing would probably be the schedule and traveling. The schedule, coming from midget, where you practice a couple times a week and play 40 games, and then when you come to the "W" and play over 70 games and practice every day; that's the toughest thing to get used to.

HP: Many players seem to comment that the hardest adjustment when joining major juniors is on the defensive end of the rink. As a defenseman, what was a major difference you noticed?

JF: Yeah, for sure. In minor hockey, you can always kind of rely on your skill, but when you get up the CHL level, you need to know all your systems so you are able to react to everything
HP: So, what would you say are some of your strengths on the ice?

JF: My best strength I would say would be my grittiness. I hate to lose. And, I'm a good skater.

HP: What about what you want to improve on?

JF: Quickness off the line. I'm working on that a lot on that this summer. And all strength and skating is huge; working on agility and bulking up to get heavier.

HP: Who were some of the tougher forwards to play against this season?

JF: Brandom MacMillan was really good off of Kelowna. Also, Brandon Kozun on Calgary was really tough to play against as well.

HP: Did you find yourself learning a lot just by playing with some of the older D-men in the W?

JF: Yeah, when you play against guys you notice certain things they do right. Some move the puck well and you want to take those aspects from them, and there are others who are solid shut down guys and you try and take some elements from them as well.

HP: Are there any NHL players you look up to?

JF: I like how Dion Phaneuf plays. He plays physical and gets points too.

HP: So what are some of your goals next season?

JF: I want to take on more of a leadership role as a 17 year old. I want to put up better offensive numbers, help out in that category. I also need to make sure that I'm reliable in all situations; the power play, penalty kill, and all of that.

HP: What about the draft? Any nerves or is it too early to think about that?

JF: Yeah, I really have tried to focus on what's next, which would be this upcoming season. But, sometimes I think about it and it's kind of nerve-wracking. But, it is also really exciting to know that I may have the chance to be drafted by an NHL team.

HP: So, what is your finest hockey memory in your career?

JF: I would say my most memorable moment would be the home opener this year. Coming out in the smoke and the lights off makes you realize you made the WHL.

HP: If you were an animal, what kind of animal would you be?

JF: If I were an animal I'd be a wolf, because I work better with a team then alone.

# Shane McColgan
## Forward - Kelowna Rockets

When talking about the most competitive players eligible for the 2011 draft, one would be remiss if they did not mention Shane McColgan. The Kelowna winger is a fiery player with a motor that never stops. He has top-flight wheels and a nice set of hands to boot. McColgan has average size at 5-foot-11, 170 pounds, but notched 25 goals and 44 assists in 71 games last season. His passion can be detrimental at times as he takes some frustration penalties. If McColgan can channel his aggression in a positive manner, he has the potential to be a dynamite NHL player.

# The Interview:

HP: So can you talk about your season very briefly?

SM: It was a good season for me personally, but as a team we did well. I think we surprised a lot of people. We made it to the second round of the playoffs, the first round was pretty tough, we played seven games with Everett, one of the hottest teams in the CHL, so I think we surprised a lot of people there. We're really excited to start next season as well.

HP: What do you think about your team's performance? I know you said before that the team surprised fans in the playoffs.

SM: I think we worked hard all season. We had to battle through a lot of adversity and we went through a streak where we lost thirteen in a row. We were losing guys, lots of guys. Actually, I've never been on a team where we've had that many injuries in one setting, so you battle through a lot of adversity and I think we had a lot of younger guys as well, so we handled ourselves well and we did well.

HP: What do you feel you bring to the team?

SM: I think I bring a lot of energy and a lot of offensive ability, but at the same time I like to focus on my own end. Being a Center man, I like to help my defense. I'm a quick guy on my feet and I like to get in those gritty areas as well, I'm a pretty gritty guy and I think I can bring the whole package.

HP: What aspects of your game have improved since you started playing in the WHL?

SM: [My game] grew tremendously, and just the speed of the game, how big the guys are and how strong they are, you just have to adjust, and I think the first couple games of the season I adjusted fine. I was out for the Memorial Cup last year and we gave that run against Windsor, and that was a great experience,

I soaked everything up. The coaching staff was great, they taught me a lot and I think that really helped me throughout the season.

HP: Like you said, there are lots of big, strong defenseman out there, and you're not a very big guy, you're 5'10" right?

SM: Yeah.

HP: So, how do you deal with big, strong defensemen coming at you?

SM: I've been training really hard for the past four years, it's benefited me, and like you said; I'm not a very big guy. When one of those big D-men come at me down low, I just use my agility and speed to get away from them and I think I'm a pretty strong guy as well, if they try to check me, I can put a body on them. I think I proved myself last season and I'm just looking for a lot better season next year.

HP: Who's helped you in your skill development the most thus far?

SM: To be honest with you, it's been mostly my natural ability and my Midget coach Jack Bowkus, he's really helped me out with my on-ice skills; with my hands and feet. I'm just always trying to get better in those areas. Honestly, I've just been working on my skill by myself and like I said, with my Midget coach, I take lessons with him pretty much every day when I'm off, taking my break. It's been good for the past three years and I think he's really helped me.

HP: How would you compare your rookie season to the one this past season?

SM: I played four games regular season and then four playoffs two years ago. I think just being one of the main guys this season. I had more experience, and I felt more comfortable around the guys, and the coaching staff, I felt more part of the team. They really helped me feel like it, and that's a big part of it.

HP: Can you speak a little bit about going up against WHL defensemen one-on-one?

SM: One-on-one, I think I'm a pretty tough player to play against. I try to work on that as much as I can, but in the league it's pretty tough to beat a defensemen one-on-one because all the defensemen are very well rounded. Sometimes you get through and you get a little lucky there, but I try to limit my game, and use my skill, and sometimes just take the easy route and taking it wide.

HP: What's been the highlight of your WHL career so far?

SM: So far, I'd say probably not playing, but watching, the Memorial Cup when we made that run against Windsor. I think that was a great experience for me, and obviously winning rookie of the year for my team, that was pretty cool, but I think probably watching the Memorial Cup.

HP: What did you learn from watching the Memorial Cup and watching your team go against Windsor?

SM: It's just getting all the experience and learning from these guys, we have over four players playing in the NHL right now from that Memorial Cup team, so I just learned a lot from them, just about the game itself, what to do, and how I can do better when I play.

HP: Do you have any personal goals for the upcoming season?

SM: I'd love to have more goals this season, we're losing a few guys, so this means the coaching staff wants me to be a leader, and I want to be a leader as well. I want to be a guy that guys look to for anything; on the ice, or off the ice. I want to make a longer playoff run and go to the Memorial Cup, that's every kid's dream. I want to ultimately go for the Stanley Cup, but the Memorial Cup is the first step and I really believe in this group.

HP: That being said, do you see yourself as a leader?

SM: Yeah, I do see myself as a leader, even though I'm a younger guy I can bring that. I think that's what the coach wants next year, and that's my goal, not to be the captain, but just a captain on the team. I think I can really bring that role on.

HP: What sorts of things motivate you?

SM: Everything. Everything motivates me, I'm that type of guy on and off the ice. I think it's just the passion I have for the game and just to be where I am right now is because of the passion and love for the game. If I didn't love the game, I don't think I could be where I am right now. I like working hard and it's going to be fun where I'm going to be in the next couple of years.

HP: You're a really pesky player and you like to get under other players' skin. Would you agree that is accurate?

SM: I think that's just the type of nature that I have and I don't care if the guy's 6'5" or 6' or 5'11", I don't care, I'll finish my check on him, I'll try to piss him off as much as he pisses me off to be honest. [laughs] I try to channel my energy and channel my emotions, and try to not let them get under my skin, but if they do, it's just the odd time and I'm not afraid to stick up for myself.

HP: What's your biggest asset?

SM: I'd probably say my speed, my coach would always tell me to use my speed to go wide. Like I said, it's hard to beat a guy one-on-one, so I try to make one move and try to beat him wide. I think I have a pretty good shot and good hands, but definitely my biggest asset is my speed.

HP: What are some of your weaknesses and things you're looking to improve on?

SM: One of my biggest weaknesses is probably channeling my emotions, I think it really showed in playoffs, guys trying to get under my skin and it frustrated me a little bit. I think it showed in the twenty-two penalty minutes I had in playoffs. It's getting a lot better to be honest with you, but you can always work on that. It's the main thing I want to work on.

HP: Can you speak a little bit about your linemates?

SM: I played with Brandon McMillan and Geordie Wudrick for most of the season, and then I played with Callahan and Brett Bulmer. I stuck with the same guys pretty much all year, but sometimes it switched because of the coach's feelings, so it always fluctuates, but it's pretty much the same guys all season.

HP: Those are great players. How do you think McMillan and Wudrick add to your game?

SM: They helped me a lot, McMillan and Wudrick were great for me this season, they helped me out a lot. I think that's why I did so well, because I played with good players and a great team by me, and that's really important.

HP: How involved does your agent get? Or do you just talk to him when there's a problem?

SM: He's really involved with me, he lives right here in L.A. The agency is close to me, so I go down there quite a bit to have lunch with him and meetings with them. If there's a problem, obviously they're here for me, and I can call them. It's not just if you have a problem, they want to know how you're doing and how you're getting treated, just stuff like that, they ask about your billet family and stuff like that. Agents are suppose to be there for you and mine's doing a really good job of doing that, so they're very involved.

HP: Is there an NHL player you would compare your play to?

SM: I think right now probably Matt Duchene. I've been compared to him a little bit, but I have a long way to go to match what he's done in the NHL, but I think we play pretty similar. He has pretty good speed, I have pretty good speed, we're about the same size, maybe he's a bit taller than me. We're both pretty strong, but I think we play a pretty similar game down low and we have a competitive edge and stuff like that.

HP: Okay, let's pretend I'm an NHL GM and I ask you "Shane, in 15 seconds, tell me why I should draft you...GO!"

SM: I think you should draft me because I'm a good character guy and leader off the ice. I'm a good offensive guy in the zone and I think when you draft me it's an investment, and to be honest I think I'm a good investment for you to have. I just bring it every night and try to be consistent and be a good person.

# Tyler Wotherspoon
## Defense – Portland Winterhawks

Tyler Wotherspoon opened up the second round at the 2008 Bantam Draft as a selection of the Portland Winterhawks (23rd overall). Tyler impressed the Winterhawks management at training camp, where his play was compared to the current team's veterans, and it was evident he was WHL material. However, due to his age(15), he was limited to a few games.

The following year Tyler was selected to play for Team Pacific at the prestigious World Under-17 Hockey Challenge alongside current Portland Winterhawks teammate Ty Rattie. Following up to the tournament and after the tournament, Wotherspoon played 43 games for the Winterhawks, where he notched one goal and totaled 5 points, along with 21 PIM.

The speedy defenseman has shown a solid performance in his own end. He's a big body and bases his game around speed. At the same time, he displays leadership characteristics and handles pressure well.

## The Interview:

HP: So Tyler, you're from Surrey. Is that correct?

TW: Yes, that's right, from the Fraser Heights area, right across the bridge.

HP: Okay, well I know hockey's pretty big in Surrey, you guys also have a BCHL franchise down in South Surrey. How did you start playing hockey?

TW: I started playing hockey when I was about seven, it was probably my first recreational year. I started skating when I was probably four or five, and I played for Cloverdale all my life.

HP: so you had the opportunity to play for Team Pacific alongside teammate Ty Rattie in the Under-17 Hockey challenge in 2009, what did that mean to you and what did you bring back from the experience?

TW: It meant a lot, seeing two of us, especially for Ty; he had a great tournament, he was our leading scorer. We showed a lot _ for our future, we had a good team, and even going there we grew a lot as players, and just playing at that level of competition with lots of players your age, shows how good the age group can be, and how well we played, and it kind of developed because it shows us how we range within our age group, it was a really good competition.

HP: You just finished a pretty busy season, how would you say your game has developed from the beginning to the present day?

TW: I felt we had a good season, I think I had a good rookie season. Over the season I've developed a lot, and gained tons of confidence. A big part of my game is playing at a high level, and I think my whole game improved; practicing every day, and playing those games, my whole game has improved.

HP: How well have you adjusted to the WHL?

TW: It's pretty hard at first, getting used to the speed and the size, but I just went along. Going to the practices, you get comfortable with it, so I've adjusted pretty well

HP: What are one or two things you think make you differ from other players in the league?

TW: I feel like I improve almost every day, I just look like I can make the first pass and it's the real key and a big part of my game; the first pass and getting it out of the zone. I feel like every year, I make huge improvements on my game, and I can see that in the future; just getting better every single day.

HP: That being said, do you see yourself as the type of player that gets things going?

TW: Yeah I'd say so. I'd say that I can see myself doing that. In a couple of years or maybe next year, becoming a role player. What's key is just getting that first pass and moving the puck forward, so I think I can see myself contributing to that.

HP: Have you taken on any leadership roles on your team?

TW: I think everybody is somewhat of a leader on our team because we're such a young team, so we all kind of help each other out by trying the best we can. Being a rookie it's hard to lead, but I know next year it'll be a much different experience in helping out the rookies for next year. Everybody's always trying to be a leader out there.

HP: You're a big guy, how do you use your size to your advantage on one on ones?

TW: Just adjusting to the speed; it's a lot faster. Also, always just trying to take the body and force the player to the outside as much as possible. If you have the wrong speed, they're just going to go right by you, so I just kind of play it soundly, getting a big gap is huge for me.

HP: Who would you say is one of the hardest forwards to go against one on one?

TW: This year one of the hardest is probably Prab Rai because he's so quick in the neutral zone and he can adjust his speed, so he's probably one of the toughest guys I've played.

HP: So, when you're in possession of the puck and you're trying to move it up, what do you think is most important; quick feet, or long strides?

TW: Nowadays, it's kind of both, but I'd say quick feet are huge, especially for D because everyone comes back and forth. I'd probably say quick feet are huge nowadays because of the quickness of the forwards.

HP: What sorts of things did you learn from your mistakes? And what do you learn from your experiences?

TW: I've learned a lot of stuff over the years, especially from the older guys, a lot about composure on the ice and feeling comfortable and not being nervous and having a lot of confidence on the ice. The biggest step from what I saw was just being confident and being smooth, and when playing, just settling down out there and making the easy play first.

HP: What sorts of things motivate you?

TW: My motivation is probably getting in the hype of the game, a lot different from what I was last year. I think just the love of the game motivates me, I love playing every day. Just [playing strong] for the team, I kind of just love the game and go out there and play my hardest every shift. I'm doing it for all the people who've helped me, so that really inspires me to play the game every day.

HP: How does that add to your confidence?

TW: Just knowing that I have the capability of doing it, I know I've done it before. I don't think about it too much and that helps me out; not thinking about it and just doing it, doing what I know I can do.

HP: What do you focus on during practice?

TW: This year, I kind of just worked on everything, I kind of worked on improving my game, but overall I'd probably say quick feet and speed because now the game's changed so much and now speed is a big part of the game. I'd say our team is very big and mobile, so I try to work on my quick feet and on my shot, and passes out of the zone.

HP: Do you base your game around speed?

TW: Yeah

HP: So you had the chance to play two playoff games for the Winterhawks this year, what were they like?

TW: I played a defensive role, just trying to make the simple plays, get it into the boards, play simple, try to make really small mistakes, try not to think about it, but just jumping into the play as much as you can and play a solid defensive game; simple.

HP: So you definitely have a lot to offer an NHL organization that's looking to draft you next year, is there anything you want from an organization in regards to your development?

TW: Nah, I just think that playing another year is going to be great, and we're going to have a great team, especially learning from the guys that are going through the draft this year, just watching them has prepared you a lot. I've seen what they have to go through and it makes you learn a lot from it for next year and it helps just watching them get through it, so it's helped a lot.

HP: What type of things do you learn from veteran players on your team?

TW: Just handling the pressure, being calm and being focused. You have to be mature, to really do it. So just watching them being focused and getting ready for the games and always practicing, working on stuff, repetitions, staying on the ice a little bit later, working on what they need to get done, and always getting better and never giving up.

HP: Here's a question to get you ready for the NHL combine next year, if you were a vegetable in a salad, how would you and the other vegetables get out of the bowl?

TW: It's got to be a team effort. You can't have just one individual trying to get out. You need to have everyone working together. You can't have one on one because that's just going to bring you down. So if everyone's working together everyone's going to get out. It's the same with our team; if everyone's working together we're going to have a good outcome.

# Ty Rattie
## RW – Portland Winterhawks

Ty Rattie was drafted by the Portland Winterhawks 2nd overall at the 2008 WHL Bantam Draft, after completing an impressive season in the Alberta Major Bantam Hockey League, where he shattered two all-time league records when he earned 75 goals and 131 points.

The following year, Ty saw much more action as he entered the Alberta Midget Hockey League and put up 29 goals and 25 assists, adding up to 54 points, in 34 games. Ty then joined Team Pacific alongside current teammate Tyler Wotherspoon in the Under-17 Hockey Challenge, where he was Team Pacific's leading scorer. It didn't stop there for Rattie; he was given the opportunity to take his game to the next level for the Winterhawks, where he had no trouble finding his scoring touch, and managed to score a goal in the 10 games he played for the team.

The Airdrie, Alberta native suited up for the Winterhawks the following year for the 2009-2010 season, where he earned a regular spot on the team., contributing 17 goals and 37 points in 61 games. In what you could call his rookie season, he made it clear that he hasn't lost his scoring touch.

# The Interview:

HP: You had a pretty solid season, who or what would you credit for your success?

TR: Well, I came in knowing we had two NHL experienced coaches, Mike Johnston and Travis Green. Obviously they were a huge part. Throughout the whole staff, the strength conditioning coach or anyone like that can help you out. A lot of it goes to the staff.

HP: How has the Winterhawks organization helped you develop your game?

TR: They're definitely a first class organization. They keep track of our off-season progression, they know what we're doing off the ice, they know what we're doing on the ice, in the summer, and it's just a first class organization.

HP: Where do you see yourself five years from now?

TR: I think I'm going to have a strong year next year and I'll have to see where the draft takes me. I think that five years from now I want to have a shot at the NHL. If not, I just want to play the highest [level] of hockey I can.

HP: What's your biggest strength on the ice?

TR: I think my offensive play. I think I can put the puck in the net, but at the same time I can take care of my defensive zone too.

HP: Can you speak a bit about your play away from the puck?

TR: It's based on what the coach thinks. If you're playing a certain game plan, you need to support the puck here, play on the defensive side etc. You just have to follow back to your own end and try to keep them out of your end.

HP: What kind of things do you need to improve on in your game?

TR: I think in the summer I'm looking to gain an extra ten pounds, I think I got pushed around too much out there last year, so gain weight. I think my game away from the puck as well; I think I have to be more aware, so I'm going to work on that this summer.

HP: You're listed at 6'0, is that correct?

TR: Yes

HP: And 170 pounds, how would you say that's impacted your game, is it a good thing, a bad thing?

TR: You could look at it both ways. I went in last year as a first year player and didn't know what to expect. I definitely know now that you need to be a good weight, a good 180 going into that because there are bigger, stronger, older players out there. Last year was a big eye opener for me, so I'm definitely going in next year with more experience.

HP: Well, you aren't a small guy, you're six feet, you have a pretty good frame. How do you use your body to your advantage?

TR: I think you just have to use your speed, keep your feet moving out there. Try not to get hit too much. If you look at the best players in the NHL, they're not always the biggest guys, but they keep their feet moving. You just have to keep your feet moving out there and you should be fine.

HP: Do you have any goals for next season?

TR: Yeah, I think I'm going into next season trying to be a top draft pick. Personally, I want to try to be a top draft pick, but then I think of the team. We think we can top what we did last year. We think we can make a push to the WHL championships.

HP: Where do you see yourself getting drafted? You said you want to be a top draft pick, so where do you see yourself in the draft?

TR: I think anywhere in the first round would be a huge honor. I think that's what I'm going into the next season with; the mindset of going in the first round. I just have to keep that mindset for the whole year and hopefully it'll push me there.

HP: What's been the highlight of your Western Hockey League career so far?

TR: It's definitely got to be game seven of our first round against Spokane. Going into OT, I scored the game winner goal. I think it was probably the best goal of not only my WHL career, but my whole hockey career.

HP: Is there an NHL player you compare your game to?

TR: I like to watch Jason Spezza from Ottawa quite a bit. I think me and him have the same low skating stride. I think Spezza has a good set of low skating strides and I pattern my stride alongside him.

HP: So would you say you focus more on long strides or quick feet?

TR: I think it depends where you are on the ice. If you're going up and down the ice, you have to have long strides, but if you're in the end or in your own end you need quick feet and get to puck as fast as you can.

HP: Okay Ty, pretend I'm an NHL GM. I'll give you 15 seconds to tell me why I should draft you.

TR: Well I think I could compete hard at the net, I know how to play the game. I'll do whatever it takes to win for the team and I think I'm a team player. Just tell me what to do and I'll do it.

HP: Okay, so here's just a fun question to get you ready for the combine. Let's say you and your teammates are out on a road trip and you're late for curfew. There's only one taxi available that can only take four players. You have the money, what do you do?

TR: That's a tough one. I think at that point, if we're all late, you got to call the coach and just let him know that you're going to be a little bit late and we'll take the punishment. Then at that point just let the guys go, and then myself as well as whoever is left go after the [taxi]. Then just take the punishment the next day, whatever the coach has in for you.

# Graeme Craig
## Defense – Swift Current Broncos

Swift Current Broncos' Graeme Craig was drafted 64th overall in the 2008 Bantam Draft as a graduate from the Red Deer North Star Chiefs. Despite planning to suit up for the Okotoks Oilers in the AJHL, he found himself with the Broncos after an impressive performance at training camp.

The Red Deer, Alberta native recently completed his rookie campaign with the Broncos as a 16 year old, and has already made a footprint in the locker room and on the ice. Playing 61 games as a rookie with the Broncos, he's gained valuable experience and posted 8 points with 31 PIM to go along with it.

Graeme has gained a lot of respect around the league with his 6'4" stature and his ability to use his size to his advantage. The stay at home defenseman brings success to his team with his strong, solid, and tough performance in his own end and in the corners.

**The Interview:**

HP: So Graeme, what was going through your mind when the Broncos drafted you at the Bantam Draft in '08?

GC: I was pretty excited that day. Actually, I was playing and was in the third period and somebody called me and told me that I got picked by the Broncos. I was excited because my brother got picked there too, but he ended up going the NCAA route. I wasn't sure what I wanted to do yet, but knew I wasn't going to leave them (Swift Current) out of the picture.

HP: You just finished your first season in the Western Hockey League, how would you say your game has improved from the beginning of the season to present today?

GC: Basically, everything I think. Definitely passing, you have to pass a lot harder than Midget. Skating too, there are some pretty fast guys in the league. You just get better, you play with a lot of older guys, they have a lot more experience and you can watch them. Your defense in the zone and coverage gets a lot better, you learn how to block more shots and get in passing lanes and all that kind of stuff. I thought I improved, my parents as well, they thought I improved a great deal by the end of the year.

HP: Just adding to what you said, what sort of things do you learn from the older players on your team?

GC: Controlling the play, I'd say is a big one. You watch them play against those top guys. A guy like [Matt Tassone] on our team, he's a twenty year old and watching him play against Eberle or Schenn. You get to see how [the older players] put themselves in a line, they block shots, they're excellent in their own end. You pick up on all the things they do, their hard work, all that stuff and you can put it into your game.

HP: Do you see yourself as the type of guy that would pass that on to younger players in the years to come?

GC: I hope so. Anytime a young player comes up, if you're doing your job, hopefully they'll look at you, and probably will lead by example. I'd love to do that actually, help a younger player develop better, and hopefully he can keep on going in hockey.

HP: You're a pretty aggressive guy on the ice. How do you deal with guys trying to get under your skin, do you try to ignore them at first? Or do you just go after them once they begin to get on your nerves?

GC: If they give me a cheap shot, I don't really like taking that kind of stuff. I'll try to run them in the corner. In front of the net, I'm going to try to be more aggressive this year, maybe throw a few sticks there, try to get under theirs. We'll see how that works. As for guys trying to get under my skin, I just try not to let it bug me, but sometimes they can. But if I get them in a corner, I give them a good shot, and hopefully they go away.

HP: Who would you say are some of the biggest pests in the league? The guys that try to get under your skin?

GC: In Saskatoon they have a lot of those guys. Like McNaughty and Inglis, they're good at that. I don't know too much about the west, but I hate playing against Saskatoon. That's pretty much one of the only biggest ones; Saskatoon.

HP: Head Coach and General Manager Mark Lamb has described you simply as a "big, solid, and strong defenseman." We see you as a stay at home defenseman at this point of your career, but how do you see yourself? What type of player are you?

GC: I'd agree with what Mark said there. I like staying at home, I'd like to think I'm pretty solid in my own end, I try to hammer guys when I can. This year hopefully I'll be able to shut down other teams' top lines and maybe contribute on the powerplay. [Mark Lamb] hit it right on target there.

HP: You're a pretty big guy, how much time do you spend on conditioning and working out?

GC: During the year, I do a fair amount of weight press and that sort of stuff. I started training a week after our season ended, so I've been going for about two months now and I'll continue until camp. Fitness is just an important part of my game, you got to train or else you're not going to get better. I want to get out early this year, hopefully get in pretty good shape, build a lot of muscle, make an impression next year with the scouts, and maybe get my name called at the draft.

HP: How do you use your size to your advantage?

GC: Getting in the corners you have to protect the puck there, out-strength guys. If they get their stick on the puck, you get under theirs and hopefully knock them off. So in the corners protecting the puck and that kind of stuff.

HP: You had the chance to play one playoff game for the Broncos, was the experience any different from a regular season game?

GC: Yeah, the atmosphere in the rink. Even though we were playing in Regina that game, we had a lot of fans come out. The atmosphere was really intense, especially in that last game where we went to OT. It was a disappointment to lose, especially since we got so close this year. It was a lot different, warm up was more intense, and watching the game from the bench, it was a lot faster and you could see guys really wanted to win, and after they scored that OT winner, it was a disappointment.

HP: You've just finished a season and had the chance to see your peers play and acknowledge what they're capable of. Where do you see yourself going in the draft and why?

GC: I've never actually heard any rankings or anything, so wherever I go, I know I'll be happy to go. If I'm the last pick of the draft, I'll be excited to go to whatever team picks me. It's an honor to play in the NHL and not many guys get to do it. Not everyone gets drafted, so wherever I go, I'll be satisfied.

HP: Okay, let's pretend I'm an NHL GM and I ask you; 'Graeme, in 15 seconds, tell me why I should draft you...GO!'

GC: I'm a big body, I can use my body to my advantage, mobile skater, see the ice well, I can pass the puck, good first pass, hard shot, and can even shut down a top line.

HP: Here's a crazy question to prep you for the Combine next year. What would you do if I gave you an elephant?

GC: [laugh] If you gave me an elephant?

HP: Yes

GC: I would feed it, and buy a house for it I guess. I don't know, that's a tough question. Hopefully breed it and whoever wants an elephant can have one. I don't really have much of a need for an elephant.

# Mitch Topping
## Defense – Chilliwack Bruins

Mitch Topping of the Chilliwack Bruins was drafted 8th overall at the 2008 Bantam Draft. A young, fifteen year old Mitch Topping had just come off a very productive season as the captain of the Red Deer White Bantams AAA team in the Alberta Midget Hockey League.

The Red Deer native followed up to play a few games the following season with the Bruins, before engaging on his rookie campaign the following year. At 6'2", the physical Mitch Topping was a challenge for many forwards in the Western Hockey League, and Mitch became a regular on the team. In addition to his solid, physical game, Mitch also has offensive upside; scoring 4 goals, and contributing 9 assists to total 13 points, he earned a spot with the Bruins.

# The Interview:

HP: Can you just talk briefly about last season?

MT: It was good. Obviously we had a new coach. Marc Habscheid came in and did a great job I thought, kind of rebuilding from what I thought was a tougher season last year. We had some good leadership. It's just a stepping stone towards rebuilding. We made huge strides with the rebuilding, and we're trying to carry that on to next season.

HP: So do you think Marc Habscheid provided the players with more of a winning attitude?

MT: Yeah, for sure. Marc jolted into our heads from day one "just do anything to win." We made some steps forward and everyone helped.

HP: What do you feel you bring to the team?

MT: I've always been more of a puck moving, skating defenseman. I try and do my best at the defensive end, but the offensive upside has always been there with me. I'm really going to work on that next season, my defensive play, but I guess in general I'd say just a skating, puck moving defenseman.

HP: What aspects of your game have you improved on since you began playing in the WHL?

MT: Just quick decisions. Obviously coming out of Midget, the guys are bigger, faster, stronger. You need to move the pucks quicker. You need to just read the scene before anything happens out there. That was the biggest part, just making quick decisions and making the easy play.

HP: Can you elaborate on what you consider is involved in making quick decisions?

MT: Like where to move the puck. Guys are on you so fast, unbelievable fore-checks with some of the stronger teams, you've just got to move the puck either to your D, or up to the wall or to your winger. You just always got to be aware.

HP: Who has helped you the most in regards to skill development?

MT: I can't really credit that to one person, the coaching staff here is phenomenal, the extra stuff they do with me at practice and between games, and that kind of thing. But the older guys too, guys like Brandon Manning, Jeff Einhorn, Jesse Craig, guys like that. They've played a lot of games in the league, and just hearing what they have to say through experience is what really helps me I found too.

HP: Is there a player you look up to in the dressing room?

MT: For this year it's definitely Jesse Craig. I got asked about him a few times this year, he's the oldest guy on the team, but he was one of my better friends on the team as well. He always looked out for me, he kind of took me under his wing ever since I showed up last year. Just little pointers throughout the season, picked me up when I was down, and kept me level headed when I was up. I owe a lot to a guy like that.

HP: So he's been somewhat of a mentor to you?

MT: Yeah, pretty much. He's been kind of almost like a dad out there. He's been playing junior since he was about my age as well, and just through experience he's helped me a ton.

HP: How would you compare your performance in your rookie season, to the one this past year?

MT: Just the confidence went up for sure. Coming up as a fifteen year old last year, you get really nervous; you're young, you're stepping into the league, you're not really sure—the other guys have had a full season under them. But this year, you just get a chance to be part of practice, the daily routines, you're at school, and obviously you're playing the whole season. So as the year went on my confidence grew.

HP: So is confidence a pretty important aspect of your game?

MT: I find it really huge. Confidence is key to playing well for me. Like I said before, you've got to keep a level head, but knowing you can make that pass or get the puck on net, it's huge and that's, again, what the older guys would help me with.

HP: Who are some of the players you feel are the toughest to go against one on one?

MT: There are tons [of players] to list there. Portland had unbelievable offense with the Niederreiter-Ross-Johansen line. They were obviously one of the tougher lines to stop. Eberle's an obvious one, he's an unbelievable hockey player. We played Calgary's Brandon Kozun. The quick guys like that are shifty and you just can't read them, those are the guys that are tough to stop.

HP: What's been the highlight of your WHL career so far?

MT: I'd just say making the playoffs and just the round we had, coming off a tough season last year with the Bruins. Just being involved with the playoffs. I just like the atmosphere and coming back in some OT games and some really close games with Tri-cities. Just how close we came as a team, that was unbelievable. I've never felt anything like it, even though we did lose in the first round. But just gaining that experience and seeing what it's all about.

HP: So how important is experience to you? Because I know some players learn from their mistakes and experience, so how does experience show in your game?

MT: Well obviously experience is going to help. Next year we'll make the playoffs again, we're looking towards rebuilding, so with the experience of playoffs behind us, it's going to help us again with the confidence; we'll know what to expect, what the crowds are like, what the intensity of the game's like. So just having that under your belt is really handy. So like I said, just to know what's coming and so we can play our game.

HP: Do you have any personal goals for the upcoming season?

MT: Well yeah, but more of my goals right now are set on the summer, just to get stronger and basically make myself 'pro-ready.' Strength is a huge thing. Like I said, guys are a lot bigger, faster, stronger, and being young, I'm looking to get stronger and battle in the corners with the bigger guys. But I'd like to contribute to the team offensively next year, play a bigger role on the powerplay, and I look to get up to the top two D pairings for sure.

HP: You are 6'1", so you're not small, can you explain some of the areas where you want to "get stronger"?

MT: Well just physically stronger. All the older guys are starting to fill out and the strength in the corners is huge. I just need to work on my balance, stick strength, grip strength, just all that stuff is going to help me in my own end, so like I said before, I need to work in my own end for sure, and then strength is going to be a huge part of that.

HP: What sort of things motivate you?

MT: Just the fact that we need to win. It's pretty standard across the board with most players, just the fact of winning. You'll do anything out there to win, especially during playoffs, like the guys were going down, blocking shots, taking hits. We're going to do anything when it comes down to winning the game and that's what keeps me going as well.

HP: What are some players you really respect around the WHL?

MT: Quite a few. There's always a lot of good players and guys that have names for themselves. There are so many players you play against, but like in the playoffs against Tri-cities, you learn to respect guys. They won against us very humbly, they're a very hard working team, you learn to respect most of the guys on that team. Lazo, Reddick, Shinnimin, those guys, you learn to respect them, they worked hard and obviously made a deep run at playoffs. Specific players; there are just so many in the league that are classy individuals that you can look to be like. It's tough to name just a few.

HP: Who are some of the best chirpers, players that really try to get under your skin?

MT: Brendan Gallagher for one. We played him a ton, obviously him being in Vancouver. He likes to run his mouth, very good hockey player, but he's known to get under your skin for sure. Guys like Beach and Shane McColgan are similar, but as far as the chirping goes, I'm going to give that to Gallaghar.

HP: How involved does your agent get? Do you talk to him often or just when a problem arises?

MT: I have a healthy relationship with my agent for sure. We're very close, he's a family oriented guy and we talk on a regular basis, it's not an everyday thing by any means. My agents have been very good to me, they handle every situation I approach them with very professionally and my family and me have absolutely no complaints, they're very good individuals.

HP: You're a big guy. You spoke earlier about getting stronger but have you been able to use your size to your advantage?

MT: That's another thing I need to work on, with the strength and stuff; just body positioning, getting between the other players and the puck. Just coming out with good angles out of the corners, and stopping guys from getting to my net. Again that's where balance and strength is going to come in, the stick strength and stuff, I need to work on that for sure.

HP: So you're looking to improve on your body positioning to increase the effectiveness of your physical game?

MT: Yup, for sure. That's obviously huge, just working on my positional play for sure within our system. But that's something I'm definitely looking forward to working on this season.

HP: So what would you say are some of the real strengths of your game?

MT: Skating and passing, and my shot have always been my strengths. Like I said, I've always been more of an offensive-minded defenseman, I like to jump into the play and make outlet passes. I've always been a powerplay player. I like to quarterback the powerplay and just set things up, read the play and try to create stuff.

HP: Can you tell us about your D-partners from last season?

MT: I played with two guys this season mostly, it was Tyler Stahl and Zach Habscheid. Big tough guys, they kind of complemented my offensive rushing. Kind of were stay at home Ds and could back me up when I went into the play, so it worked out pretty well.

HP: So stay at home guys really compliment your game?

MT: Yeah, I'd say so for sure. It's always nice to have a big stay at home defenseman that can back you up when you like to jump up a lot and they're really tough players. They wouldn't let anyone mess with me out there, and just great guys off the ice as well, which helps.

HP: Mitch, let's pretend I'm an NHL GM and I tell you 'Mitch, in 15 seconds, tell me why I should draft you…Go!'

MT: First off, I'm a good skater, I've really worked on that for a long time. I'm a defenseman with an offensive upside, good shots, and can get pucks out of my own end through passing. Off the ice, I'm very motivated, coachable, and just willing to learn.

# Tyler Biggs
## Forward – USA NTDP

Biggs heads into his second USHL season after completing a solid rookie campaign. He progressed nicely as the season rolled along and won gold medals as a bonus. He won the MVP in the gold medal game in Timmons, Ontario in the world under 17 championships.

Tyler was a second draft pick in the OHL by the Oshawa Generals despite the fact that he publicly committed to the USNTDP prior to the OHL draft. Tyler has pro hockey bloodlines. His father Don played 18 seasons as a professional, including an 11 game stint in the NHL with the Philadelphia Fylers. Don Biggs played his OHL hockey in Oshawa by the way. Tyler has committed to Enrico Blasi's Miami Redhawks in the NCAA.

Biggs is a player HP knows very well as he suited up for our prospect team prior to the OHL draft in 2009. Biggs is a power forward in every way, shape and form. He can skate and plays a tough physical game. He also can, and will drop the gloves.

## The Interview:

HP: What was your first season like for the USA Team in the USHL?

TB: I think everyone expected it would get off to a bit of a slow start, and it did and we didn't get enough wins in the beginning. But, as the year went on and we hit December, as a team we really turned it around and we started taking it to the USHL teams more and more. When we ended up winning the U-17 challenge it was a huge accomplishment. Being recognized as some of the best 16 year old hockey players in the world, is a huge achievement for any player.

HP: What was the thought process like in joining the US team?

TB: Well, there are always high expectations for anyone who comes from the program; it is a highly regarded program between the coaching and training. For me, when playing in Canada I decided I wanted to play NCAA hockey and not the OHL and I realized the best step for me to get there was to join the program and start playing against much older kids night in and night out. I didn't know what to expect in the beginning, but I think my game has developed greatly and I don't regret it one bit.

HP: What were the more challenging things to adjust to this season?

TB: I think this year was a huge wakeup call for a lot of us; not being used to playing against the older and stronger competition. My dad coached a junior team so I knew a little bit what to expect. I'm also bigger which helped a lot along the way. Definitely getting used to how physical each game was and always having to push back is something I wasn't quite used to. It's been a good learning experience.

HP: If you were scouting yourself, what would you describe as your strengths?

TB: On the ice, I would say my skating and speed; I like to take defensemen wide. I also have the ability to finish around the net and obviously my competitive nature. Off the ice, I try to be coachable and carry myself professionally and that leadership presence that goes with a power forward game. Hopefully I will get a little better with stick skills and my defensive positioning.

HP: How did you go about choosing hockey, any family influences in the situation?

TB: Obviously, I think anyone whose father played professional hockey would be greatly influenced by that. But, for me in particular, his influence has been huge. He coached me from day one until about two years ago when I made the move to Toronto to play. Basically, the player I am today and my competitiveness and all that goes back to him. The grit, the competitive nature, and effort really comes from him and how he played when he was playing. I am very thankful for his influence.

HP: Are there any specific lessons you've taken from your father now that he isn't coaching you anymore?

TB: I say most of all my personality as a player. I try to be a professional and he was a major leader when he was playing, and I think I've always had and wanted that role and responsibility. Recently, I've been given that opportunity and I've taken it and ran with it this year. His leadership qualities and how he respected and cared for his teammates is something I value. In terms of our games, I think we are a bit different. He could definitely score goals and was smaller than me. I think I'm more of a power forward.

HP: Who have been some of the tougher defensemen you've gone up against in your career?

TB: I got the chance to go against Eric Gudbranson when playing in the World Championships (U-18 tourney in Belarus). He's almost impossible to knock off the puck and finishes his checks. Hitting him was like hitting a brick wall.

HP: Speaking of the U-18 tourney, as a young player, what was that experience like for you?

TB: I think it was a different situation. I just got the call up, I had no idea what to expect or what my role was. It was a huge learning experience; going from the guy to just a part of the puzzle. Eventually, I learned my role and went with it. It wasn't what I was used to, but I realized you had to check your ego at the door, and 21 other guys on the team are trying to win a world championship.

HP: It's all worth it to win, right?

TB: Yup, exactly.

HP: What would you say has improved most about your game this season?

TB: This year, I actually developed into a role. It was a more of a power forwards game, which has helped me become a more complete player. I can be counted on more in the defensive zone in big situations like the penalty kill or end of games. I grew as a player that a coach can rely on to accept a challenge.

HP: A lot of players that are just making the transition to either the major juniors or any other comparable league seem to say that it's tough at first but when you accept the challenge and a new role, you can really grow into a better player. Would you say this is how it tends to go?

TB: I think you definitely need to be challenged. The guys in Canada are going to be challenged by playing in the CHL and it was the same in the USHL. You have to find your role so you can fit and grow as a player. I think that Being challenged and finding your role is a huge part in growing as a player.

HP: What has been the most memorable moment of your playing career?

TB: I think it would have to be the U-17 challenge this year. Winning it with the guys near the end of the season was a great experience. We weren't necessarily the most talented national team program, but we were the hardest working and to go undefeated against teams like Ontario and Sweden was unbelievable. We worked our tails off and I wouldn't trade the experience for anything.

HP: What are your goals for the upcoming season?

TB: It's pretty simple; just to develop more as a player. I want to be more of an offensive player and more of a leader like I know I can be. In the end ,I would say it has to be winning a world championship.

HP: What was the decision process like in choosing Miami to play NCAA hockey? How did you go about choosing to play college hockey and then Miami specifically?

TB: I think I have a great relationship with the coaching staff there. It didn't develop as much until later in the season as I started talking to them more and more. Even though it was a school in my backyard, it wasn't the highest on my radar until I went on my visit. A lot of guys say that when you go on your visit, you sometimes can just tell if it's the right fit, and that's the way it was with Miami. I feel like I'll fit in great and so will my game.

HP: Who are some players you like to watch either in major juniors, NCAA, or NHL?

TB: I think there are a couple guys in the NHL. A couple guys would be guys like Dustin Brown, he's a good leader, led the NHL in hits despite not being the biggest guy. He brings it every night. Also, Jarome Iginla who is the ultimate leader and plays the power forward position well.

HP: If you could pick one player in the NHL whose role you could take right now, who it would be?

TB: Wow, there are a ton of options there. I guess with my power forward role, so I think more than anyone I'd go with Jarome Iginla. He's a great a player, a great vet, and will be in the NHL for a long while. He is a role model and I would take a lot of pride in filling that role.

HP: So, fast forward to the 2011 draft, if a scout is telling a GM to draft you, what is he saying to convince him? What about your game sticks out the most?

TB: Hopefully because I'm a guy who is never going to quit. I don't think I've ever been the best player on any team I've been on. I was a bit awkward [physically] when I was growing up so I had to work for everything I got. Now, I've grown into my body a bit, which works well with my work ethic. I'm going to work as hard as I can night in and night out, practice hard, and bring all of that to the table with some leadership as well. I think I take pride in a power forward role, and I want to have my teammates back; I love to drop the gloves when I can as well.

# Alan Quine

## Forward – Kingston Frontenacs

Alan Quine was the second player taken in the 2009 OHL Priority selection. The Ottawa area native played his minor midget season in Toronto before being drafted to Kingston. The Fronts first round pick impressed right out of the gates .Quine delivered offensively with five goals and four assists for nine points in his first 15 OHL games. The 5'11 172 pound forward finished up the year with a solid rookie season posting 28 points.

Quine is a smart hockey player who although smaller than a Tyler Seguin, he does plays a similar style game. Alan distributes the puck well and is also able to put the puck in the net. Quine should get all the opportunity to showcase himself this coming season in Kingston.

# The Interview:

HP: What was your first season like with Kingston?

AQ: The year went well and I got off to a good start. I got comfortable early and was really enjoying myself there. I liked playing against the higher-level competition. Unfortunately sometimes you don't get the ice time you are used to but you have to learn to take the long road and be ok with sitting some things out. But, it benefits you in the long run and I learned a lot from it and took a lot from it; so hopefully that makes me better in the future.

HP: As the second overall pick in the OHL draft, did you feel any extra pressure?

AQ: Yeah, I think there was some added pressure from everybody. Sometimes it was on the ice and sometimes it was off of it. There always seems to be someone watching you, and you have to try and live up to expectations. I think I did though; I think I lived up to them for a first year player and definitely tried as hard as I could.

HP: What were the more challenging things to adjust to this season?

AQ: I believe the most challenging thing to adjust to was the more physical play of the OHL and how much physically stronger the players are compared to minor hockey. They are also much faster than in minor hockey. You have to learn different ways to get around different guys, and learn to rely on your speed more.

HP: If you were scouting yourself, what would you describe as your strengths?

AQ: I would say my strengths include willingness to compete and be productive on both ends of the ice using my speed. I like to think I'm a good centerman that knows how to be responsible but also can make something out of nothing when I get my chance. Obviously, I like the fact that I can put up points as well and be productive

HP: What improvements have you been focusing on since joining the OHL?

AQ: I'd have to say my strength and physical play. I'm working hard right now trying to get bigger and stronger. I think it is a very important part of the game so I'm working on adding some size so I can push a few guys around out there.

HP: In regards to that, what do you think most improved in your game in your first season with Kingston?

AQ: Definitely the little things. I think I have been better at staying at the system and following what the coach asks. Overall my speed and reaction time has improved since the beginning of the season and my shot has definitely gotten better as well.

HP: Where do you think you are most productive on the ice? What do you have to make sure you do every shift to stay an effective player?

AQ: I think I'm the type of guy that likes both the open ice and the corners. I like getting in there and getting into a good battle and using puck possession and protection. But, I also like to try and create some things in open ice.

HP: Who have been some of the tougher defensemen you've gone up against in your career?

AQ: There are some tough guys on every team. The top four on every team were very solid. I remember, for example, trying to get around John Moore was tough. But, you got to watch guys and try and learn how to get around them and go from there.

HP: What are your goals for the upcoming season?

AQ: Well, in terms of goals for next season, I would say definitely getting better in all areas of the ice. I want to keep working hard, competing, upping the physical game and hopefully the points and production come from there.

HP: Who are some players you like to watch either in major juniors, NCAA, or NHL?

AQ: I try to model my game after Sidney Crosby, as much as I can. I know it's a tough thing to do but I really admire the way he plays. In the OHL, I really like the way Tyler Seguin plays. I like to play as much as I can like him. He is a good player to look up to and learn from. I've been compared to him before and I really like the way he plays and sees the ice.

HP: What similarities do Crosby and Seguin share that draws you to both of them?

AQ: I'd say they are both really good two-way players that see the ice really well and work on making players better around them.

HP: If you could pick one player in the NHL whose role you think you could play in the future, who would it be?

AQ: I'd take Jonathon Toews' role. I'd take it because he is a tremendous leader and knows what it takes to win a hockey game. Obviously, he showed it all throughout the playoffs, being the captain of the Blackhawks and showing it all over the ice. His offensive skills are second to none, but he has the entire package and is such a professional.

HP: What is the most memorable moment of your hockey career so far?

AQ: My most memorable moment would definitely be game seven this year in the first round. We didn't come out on top, but it was something special to pack our building and get everyone excited. Unfortunately, we did not quite perform up to expectations but the experience is something I'll always remember.

HP: How excited are you to have completed a year in the OHL and have that experience going into next season?

AQ: Yeah, it's good having a year under your belt. It is good to have the experience and knowledge about what happens at the level and makes it much easier to prepare for a new full season.

# Tyler Hansen
## Defense – Kamloops Blazers

Tyler Hansen was drafted 3rd round (66th overall) by the Kamloops Blazers, the third round pick originally belonged to Tri-City. The following season, the Blazers signed Hansen after having played a few games of "AAA" Midget hockey in Lethbridge.

The Magrath, Alberta native didn't have much exposure at a young age, but whenever he was granted the opportunity to put his talent on display, he did. He was eventually rewarded with the opportunity to play one game for the Blazers the same year he played AAA Midget in Lethbridge. The stay-at-home defenseman earned himself 48 appearances for Kamloops the following year, where he found success in using his size to his advantage, with a combination of speed and mobility.

# The Interview:

HP: How did you feel when you were drafted by the Blazers?

TH: I felt pretty good. I hadn't even talked to the Blazers at all, but my friend's uncle was looking for a coaching job there, so he told me that there was a really sweet program out there. So when I got drafted I got really excited to talk to some people I knew out there and they said it was a good town, good fans, and the teams haven't been too successful lately, but they're looking a lot better so I was really excited when I got drafted by them.

HP: Are you happy so far? Have they met your expectations?

TH: Yeah, I'm happy so far. I went there last summer and wasn't sure if I'd make the team though, but when I did I actually got quite a bit of playing time and a lot of chances to show my stuff. The coaches put a lot of trust in me from day one. It wasn't always so smooth; I was a healthy scratch a couple times. But overall it was really good for me and I learned a lot.

HP: You're a pretty big guy at 6' 3", how do you use your size do your advantage?

TH: You got to definitely take advantage of it, and use it to hit, but not all guys like to hit, so you definitely got to be able to hit when you're my size, and be able to push guys around, it's something they notice. The biggest thing is you got to work on your skating and your mobility when you're a big guy.

HP: How much of your game depends on your physical strength?

TH: I think that's where most of my game lies, I'm not one of the biggest offensive guys and goal scorers, mine's mostly a shut down defenseman, who plays tough and works hard.

HP: Who are some of the best chirpers out there? You know, guys that try to get under your skin.

TH: I'd say Mitch Callahan from Kelowna, and Lance Bouma, those are the top two that come to my mind.

HP: How do you deal with guys like that?

TH: For me, I'm not one of the biggest chirpers in the league, so I kind of just ignore it, get my two bits when I can, but by the play that I do. Once in a while, you got to say something back to get at them.

HP: What type of player are you? Director of Player Personnel Matt Recchi described you as "a strong young defenseman with a right-hand shot, is good in his own end, has very good mobility, and solid offensive abilities." Would you agree? How do you see yourself?

TH: I'd agree with that. I'd say that for my size, I'm getting better at mobility as I'm growing into my body more. I think that I'm a fairly tough kid, and that I work hard and don't take anything for granted.

HP: How do you think you differ from other players in the league?

TH: I think one of the biggest things for me is I came from a small town, I didn't have a lot of exposure at a young age and didn't really know about the league and what it really takes to play at higher levels when I was young. I came into an elite program at a later age, so I've really been learning how much dedication it takes to play at the higher levels, plus I didn't really have too much contact with people that had played at the higher level, so I've had to catch up with the others and learn how to prepare and what to do to get to the next level.

HP: Does that affect how well you adapt? Have you adapted well to the WHL despite not having played at the higher level before?

TH: Yeah, it was tough for me. I hadn't really talked to anyone who had played in the WHL before, so I kind of went in not knowing what to expect. I just had to take it day by day and I had to learn a lot, just by myself; asking question, experiences. It was tough to start, but it's definitely good to get that rookie year out of the way.

HP: Are there any guys in the locker room that you look up to and that have helped you out?

TH: I think the biggest leader for me is our captain; Ryan Funk. He's a really good guy in the room, he didn't look down on anyone and has been a really good teacher, leader and just a guy who would lighten the mood anytime.

HP: What are some of your strengths?

TH: My strengths would probably be defensive work, skating, playing tough, blocking shots, just doing the gritty things that D-men do.

HP: So then are you a stay at home defenseman?

TH: Yeah, that's how I consider myself.

HP: What are some weaknesses you have that you're trying to improve on?

TH: Today, stick handling, and patience with the puck; trying not to rush things too much and seeing the ice better, taking advantage of the time I do have, and making a good play from there.

HP: What aspects of your game do you work on during practice?

TH: I work on a lot of skating. I transition and stick handle the puck while moving from forward to backwards. I also work on my shot a lot too.

HP: Do you base your game around your skating?

TH: Yeah, I try to. If you take a look at the guys at an elite level, they're all great skaters, so I definitely try to focus on my skating as much as possible.

HP: Who are some of the hardest guys to stop one on one?

TH: I'd say Brett Connolly is pretty tough. Craig Cunningham, Brandon McMillan. All those guys are speedy.

HP: What are you looking most forward to this year?

TH: I'm looking forward to going back and having a chance to be a veteran this year, don't have to pack the bus and all that stuff. Have the chance to get noticed, and have the opportunity to get drafted next year.

HP: Have you taken on any leadership roles on your team this year?

TH: I think I can definitely take a bigger role. I wasn't the most talkative guy last year, just kind of listened and learned, but now that I've had the experience of learning from older guys, I think I can carry that on to the younger guys on the team—even the older guys. Anyone can always tell guys what they need to do, and just give positive criticism.

HP: What sort of things do you learn from experience? Do you learn by watching? By being told what to do?

TH: Yeah, I learned from both ways this year. I learned both by watching games when I was scratched or playing. I learned what you need to do in a certain situation, analyzing the play, and watching the puck with certain D-men; like the top D-men in the league, and what they do at certain times. I try to work on those things at practice and try to enroll them into my game.

HP: Is there an NHL player you would compare yourself to?

TH: I try to play like a Shea Weber, kind of a big tough D-man, who is physical and has a hard shot.

HP: Do you work out a lot?

TH: Yeah, I go to training five or six times a week. It's a very good every day thing.

HP: Have you been keeping up with it during the summer?

TH: Yeah, I've been pretty confident since the season ended, so I've been good.

HP: What do you think you can bring to an NHL organization that chooses to draft you?

TH: I'd say I can bring a shut down game; like shut down other lines. I can play tough, and play a long hard minute and battle in the corners, and win all my battles.

# Kale Kessy
## Defense – Kamloops Blazers

Kale Kessy debuted with the Tigers in early 2009 as a listed player, previously being a member of the Medicine Hat Midget AAA Tigers. Despite only playing 9 games in his first year, the hard-nosed centerman displayed potential.

The following season, Kale proved many critics wrong as he suited up for the Medicine Hat Tigers for 70 games. Kessy became an ultimate checking machine as he used his big body and speed to his advantage on the forecheck. At the same time, he scored 11 goals and contributed 18 assists to earn some numbers on the scoreboard for the Tigers. Kale's hybrid play earned him a spot alongside some of the elite players on the team such as Emerson Etem.

# The Interview:

HP: Can you tell us a little bit about how last season went for you and the Blazers?

KK: I thought we had a good season. We had a great group of guys, great leadership within the room and I thought the season went fairly well. We lost to Calgary, but I thought we had a good enough team, and I thought we played really hard throughout the playoffs, and I thought we had a really good season throughout the whole year.

HP: What about your role, what part did you play last season?

KK: I like to be that energy guy within the room and just work hard; shift in, shift out. Work hard on and off the ice, try to keep going and maybe chip in here and there with a goal or two.

HP: Talk about being the energy guy? Can you expand on that?

KK: I like to use my size to my advantage and finish my checks all around the rink whenever I can, and just play smart, disciplined hockey.

HP: What sort of things do you learn from your mistakes?

KK: I just try to reflect upon it, and try not to think about it too much. Just have a short memory and just move on. I know can do better after and fix it, and go out there next year and work harder and try not to do it again.

HP: Who or what would you credit for a successful season thus far?

KK: I'd probably have to give the most credit to my parents for who I am right now. Then my family and the coaching staff and my team mates for sure for helping me get better throughout the season. They know what I can do and expect the best out of me.

HP: How do you play some of the elite players in the league? There are some big and fast guys out there, what strategies do you use to be successful even against these elite players?

KK: There's a lot of talented players throughout the league and every team has a lot of good players, and it's harder to play against the bigger guys than the more fragile guys, but you just have to learn their weaknesses and get pucks in deep, and try to wear them down or finish up your hit.

HP: What's been the highlight of your WHL career thus far?

KK: The highlight of my career so far has been my first WHL game. Just the atmosphere that's in the building is great; there are great fans that support the team and are really into the game of hockey.

HP: What sorts of things motivate you?

KK: I'd have to say just imagining that you could be playing high level hockey one day, and just watching hockey on TV. I'd have to say that just growing up, playing hockey, working hard, and just watching hockey on TV. Watching you're favorite player play in the Stanley Cup playoffs, and one day hopefully to be there. How hard you work motivates you to be what you have to be, and how much better you have to be to get there.

HP: Who are some of the best chirpers out there? Guys that try to get under your skin?

KK: I try not to worry about them too much. I just go out there and try to play my game, and just leave them behind me and not worry about what they're trying to say, and hopefully I have nothing to say back.

HP: You're a pretty big guy, how do you use your size to your advantage?

KK: I like to finish off my checks whenever I can, get pucks in deep, and wear down their defensemen. If I have to fight, I'll fight, but I don't go looking for it. I just go out there and work hard, and whatever happens just happens.

HP: Do you have any personal goals for the upcoming season?

KK: For the upcoming season, I want to make the Tigers and hopefully when the season comes along just work hard. It's a big year for me, hopefully get drafted and maybe go to the combine.

HP: What are your strengths on the ice?

KK: I think I'm a pretty big guy out there, so I like to use my size to my advantage; I like to finish my checks. I think I'm fairly fast, and a pretty good energy guy.

HP: Then what are some things you want to improve on? Your weaknesses.

KK: Well, I think anyone could always improve on their skating, no matter what. And I think my shot, and my patience with the puck I think I could always work on.

HP: Okay so you've played with a lot of different guys, how does that affect your game? Does it really make a difference?

KK: No, I don't think who I play with really affects [my game]. Like I said before, we have a great group of guys; we work hard, so it doesn't really matter to me who I play with. When I get the opportunity to be on the ice, I just go out there and work hard, and whatever happens, it happens.

HP: Is there an NHL player you would compare your play to?

KK: I like the way Mike Richards and Milan Lucic play. They're two of my favorite players, they work hard day in day out, they both have great leadership on and off the ice, and they just got me by how hard they work throughout the game, and how hard you have to work to reach that level.

HP: Kale, let's pretend I'm an NHL GM and I ask you 'Kale, in 15 seconds, tell me why I should draft you…GO!'

KK: I think I'm a hard working player that would do anything to win, and I put the team before myself and, and just a hard-working guy that can bring energy to the team, and do whatever it takes to win a championship.

# Zach Hall
## Center – Barrie Colts

Zach Hall is both a playmaker and scorer, who works hard shift after shift  If not for a Barrie team that was pushing for a memorial cup berth last season, he would have played in the OHL last year.

Hall was a member of the Couchiching Terriers last season and finished second on his team in scoring.  Hall's numbers were impressive for a rookie: 71 pts in 44 games, including 26 goals. Hall will get plenty of ice this season but wins will be harder to find in his NHL draft year with the Colts rebuilding.

## The Interview:

HP: How did your season go with Couchiching?

ZH: It was really good. I thought I got really good coaching and we had a pretty good team as well.

HP: How did you go about choosing hockey, any family influences in the situation?

ZH: Everyone in my family played or plays hockey. My dad played for the Bulls (a junior B team) and my brother got drafted to Peterborough in 2006, and I just always have been playing. I first got on the ice when I was two and I've loved the game since.

HP: We believed you were talented enough to spend the season with Barrie, was it frustrating not to play for them?

ZH I knew we, the Colts, had a very good team and that I also was quite young. So, I took it on a positive note, and worked extra hard in Couchiching with the Terriers. I would say that it motivated me because I could so clearly see the end goal of playing with the Colts staring me in the face. Also, it was great to get to play in some games in the end.

HP: How did that small sampling with Barrie go?

ZH: It was very good. I was excited for every game and it was thrilling to play. The playoff and regular season games were both exciting and it was a great experience.

HP: What were some of the bigger differences between playing in Couchiching and Barrie?

ZH: It was a lot more high paced in Barrie. Obviously, the players were better from top to bottom. More guys competed and wanted the puck in the OHL then Junior A. it was also a lot more high tempo.

HP: How do you think having such a successful year in Couchiching will help you next season?

ZH: It was good because I got the opportunity to play a lot. I got to play on the first line, and my line-mate had tons of points, and he really helped me out a lot and gave me some great pointers.

HP: If you were scouting yourself, what would you describe as your strengths? What about some weaknesses?

ZH: My strengths are skating, vision of the ice, and my shot.

HP: What about some weaknesses you want to improve on?

ZH: I've been working on my defense and playing the body more.

HP: Where would you say you are most productive on the ice, be it in the corners, in front of the net, in transition etc...

ZH: I would say probably in transition is where I get most of my opportunities. However, I also get them in the corners as well because I find the open spot well.

HP: You mentioned that you think your strengths are your speed and shot. Do you think that is why you are so productive in the open ice?

HP: What would you say has improved most about your game this season?

ZH: Well at the beginning of the year, I kept finding myself ahead of the play; my timing just wasn't right compared to AAA hockey. I like to pride myself on being in the right place at the right time, and from the start of the season, I just wasn't content with my timing. For example, I'd be too far ahead in the breakout. But, as the season went on I think I got my timing right and adjusted better.

HP: So, it took some time to adjust to the new league so you could again work on being in the right position?

ZH: Yeah, that's correct.

HP: What has been the most memorable moment of your playing career?

ZH: So far I would have to say finally cracking my OHL team was pretty memorable.

HP: What are your goals for the upcoming season?

ZH: I'm looking forward to trying to put up 50 points or more. It's a tough question because I want to improve on everything. I guess specifically defense would be something I need to improve on.

HP: Who are some players you like to watch either in major juniors, NCAA, or NHL?

ZH: Yeah, for the last couple years I've watched Zach Parise of the New Jersey Devils. I have watched him really closely. I like watching him play because he's not the biggest guy out there but never backs down from anyone. He could be going up against Zdeno Chara and won't back down.

HP: Have you had any nerves regarding the 2011 NHL Draft?

ZH: Yeah, but only good ones. It's such an exciting thought to think that I could get drafted.

HP: So, fast forward to the 2011 draft, if a scout is telling a GM to draft you, what is he saying to convince him? What about your game sticks out the most?

ZH: I would say most likely my speed, shot, and vision. Hopefully he likes that I can always find the right spot on the ice.

HP: What is the best piece of advice you have received from a coach?

ZH: I would say not to ever think too far ahead; take everything day by day whether it's practice, a game, or working out. Pretty much don't look too far ahead or too far behind.

# Tomas Jurco
## Left Wing – Saint John Sea Dogs

Tomas Jurco is a Slovak born winger who just completed his first season in the QMJHL with the St.John Sea Dogs. The late 1992 born Jurco was fantastic as a rookie posting 26 goals and he added 25 assists. Jurco was also a big part of the Dogs long 21 game playoff run. Tomas added 7 goals and 10 assists in the playoffs which just adds to an impressive resume.

The left handed shooting Jurco is listed at 6'1 190 lbs. Jurco will showcase his speed and elite soft hands to NHL scouts leading up to next year's draft in Minnesota. If you want a preview of his skills you can visit the HockeyProspect.com video section.

## The Interview:

*Please note that Tomas has a limited grasp of the English language.*

HP: How did you decide to play in the QMJHL this season instead of staying in Europe ?

TJ: Canada is one big hockey country and I get some deals from CHL. Because I am from Slovakia and that is not that famous country in hockey world, I decided that leaving Slovakia would be better for my hockey future and also for my NHL draft.

HP: What was your first season like in St. John ?

TJ: I would say that my first season was successful, first of all I had to get used to play and all new stuff around me like smaller rink and the different kind of play but when I got used to everything my game was better and better.

HP: What are some of the strengths in your game?

TJ: I think maybe my good hands, thinking on the ice and my speed.

HP: What kind of player do you consider yourself; What is your role in St. John ?

TJ: I would say that I am a sniper, my role was to score some goals and I think that will be my same role I'll have next season.

HP: Where are you most productive on the ice? For example, in the corners, in transition, shooting the puck, etc..

TJ: I think for sure that I'm dangerous in front of the net or between the circles. I can score many goals from there.

HP: What are you trying to improve this offseason?

TJ: I am trying to improve a few things. I'm working at my power. I'm doing many drills for speed, and I need to get some kilograms on my frame.

HP: What aspect of your game has improved most since you began playing for St.John?

TJ: I think I have improved in a many areas but probably my defensive game has improved most out of all areas.

HP: We've seen you showcase some very nice moves, is that something you practice, or does it just comes naturally?

TJ: When I was younger I played with the puck every day, I was trying some trick, and this stayed with me till now but I still sometimes take a stick and play around with something.

HP: Do you have a favorite move?

TJ: I like my shootout move what I made and used once in Cape Breton

HP: Who are some of the stronger defensemen you have played against in your career?

TJ: One of the strongest defensemen is for sure Yan Sauve, but I was lucky that he was playing in my team.

HP: Do you have any Slovakian players you look up to?

TJ: I like Marian Hossa and Marian Gaborik. Those are two NHL players I look up to.

HP: What about any players in general in the NHL or CHL that you like to model your game after?

TJ: I like to watch to play Marian Hossa, and then trying to take something of his skills.

HP: What are your goals for next season?

TJ: Play at the Under 20 World Juniors in Buffalo for Slovakia National team, and maybe beat 30 goals in the Q.

HP: Do you think about or have you had any nerves about the 2011 NHL Draft, or is it too early?

TJ: Sometimes I think about draft, but it's too early and I have to think about my play, play as good as I can and then I don't have to worried about draft.

HP: Fast forward to the 2011 draft, if a GM is drafting you, why is he drafting you; what kind of player is he getting?

TJ: I think that G.M would draft me because I'm a very Fast skater and I'm sniper, I am always trying to get better. I work hard to make my skill better.

HP: If you were an animal, what kind of an animal would you be and why?

HP: I say I would be a Leopard – fast, strong and hungry

# Michael St. Croix
## Center – Edmonton Oil Kings

Michael St Croix comes from a hockey family, both his father and older brother having played professional hockey. Drafted 4$^{th}$ overall by the Edmonton Oil Kings at the 2008 Bantam Draft, he had just come off an impressive season playing for the Winnipeg Monarchs AAA Bantam team where he had notched 51 goals and 96 points in only 25 games.

The Winnipeg native led his Midget team, the Winnipeg Wild, the following year to the Manitoba Midget AAA League championship. Through the course of the year, St. Croix was also the league leader in scoring with 56 goals and 103 points in 41 games. He also received the chance to play for Team West in the Under-17 World Hockey Challenge in Port Alberni as a 15-year old.

Michael engaged on his rookie campaign in 2009, despite having played 2 games the previous season where he gathered two points including a goal in his first game. In the 66 games where St. Croix suited up for the Oil Kings, he put up 18 goals and 46 points. He returned and proceeded to re-unite with Team West for the Under-17 World Hockey Challenge in Timmins, Ontario, his second time taking part in that tournament.

## The Interview:

HP: Coming off a strong season in Manitoba, you were drafted 4th overall at the Bantam Draft in 2008, that's a pretty big honor. How did you feel and what was going through your head when you were drafted?

MSC: I think I was just very grateful and thankful for having such a great team, and a great coach; Carey Chartier. It was a pretty exciting year with some championships won, some tournaments, and being drafted by the Edmonton Oil Kings was definitely a little icing on the cake.

HP: Let's backtrack a little bit. What got you started in playing hockey? Was there another sport you played before you started playing hockey?

MSC: Well, I have a hockey family. My father played for the Toronto Maple Leafs and the Philadelphia flyers. My brother, who's almost 31 now, played hockey, got drafted to the Calgary Flames, played for the Kamloops Blazers, and has played in the American league, over in Europe. It's just a hockey family. It's what I've grown up with my whole life, and I've fallen in love with it at a very early age.

HP: What age did you start playing hockey at?

MSC: I think I was skating around four and started playing when I was five.

HP: You dominated the Manitoba Midget AAA Hockey League in scoring as a fifteen year old. You led your team to the championships and you won the championships. Who or what do you credit for the success you've had at such a young age up to now?

MSC: I would definitely have to say my family again; my dad, my brother, as well as coaches along the way—and teammates. I can't give enough credit to my coaches, especially Carey Chartier who had me for three years in Bantam; he taught me lots of things, gave me lots of advice; how to play on the defensive side, as well as some tips on scoring. I can't give enough credit to Carey Chartier. I was able to play with some great hockey players over the time; Brendan O'Donnell, he was actually just drafted to the Tampa Bay Lightning, Zachary Franko, and the list goes on of the great players I've been able to play with. Success is definitely a result of all these other people coming together to help me along the way.

HP: You're definitely a talented player. You can score goals and you're good with the puck. You really look like you know what you're doing out there, but what parts of your game are you looking to improve on?

MSC: I always want to get better at skating. It's something that in the new era of the NHL, it's such an important thing to be able to skate; skate fast, be strong on your skates. Every part of my hockey game I want to improve at, but skating, strength, and defensive play is something I'm really going to take extra effort in, in order to improve.

HP: GM Bob Green commented "Michael is the type of player who is going to adapt quickly to this league," you scored a goal in your first game when you played for the team as a fifteen year old, now that you have a full season under your belt, how would you say you've adapted to the Western Hockey League

MSC: It actually took a little bit longer than I expected to adapt. It took about 20 games, and I wasn't getting too much opportunity at the start of the year. I had to show the coaches that I was willing to do whatever it took. It took a while, I was used to going on teams and being on the first line, but it was a learning experience and once I was able to learn and show the coaches that I was willing to do what it takes, I was moved up, and I was able to play some big minutes and put up some points.

HP: And how did you show the coaches that you were willing to do whatever it takes?

MSC: It's all the little things, the little details; the little things in the defensive zone, finishing every check, making the smart playes, not trying too hard—not trying to do things you're not supposed to do. My coaches just kept telling me to focus on what I could do, and not to try to be something that I'm not, and at the end it paid off.

HP: Can you give me a scouting report on yourself?

MSC: I guess I'd say I'm a smaller forward who knows how to put the puck in the net, but also likes setting up his teammates—I like to make my teammates better around me. I'm a two-way centerman, pretty strong on my skates, pretty good skater, and I'm not afraid to mix it up.

HP: Last season, you got to see teammates like Mark Pysyk go through their draft season leading up the NHL Entry Draft, did you learn anything from watching them prepare? Like how to handle stress or stay focused, that sort of thing?

MSC: For sure! Actually, I was able to go out with my agent to the draft, which just took place in Los Angeles, and the learning experience was absolutely incredible. I was able to see some interviews, watch the draft take place, watch the trades, and especially watch Mark Pysyk, a good buddy of mine, get drafted to the Buffalo Sabres 23rd overall. Over the year, Mark showed me lots of things—showed me how to prepare for the draft. Obviously, the draft is going to be in your head, and you're going to be thinking about it many times, but putting all these emotions and the thoughts of getting drafted high, have to leave, because in all honesty, you have to be focused on playing hockey, and helping out the Edmonton Oil Kings. So, watching Mark this year with all the stress of the draft, and everything that was going on around him, it was amazing to see how he took all the individual success and acknowledgement away, and just played for the Edmonton Oil Kings.

HP: How would you say you're going to incorporate that experience towards yourself throughout your draft season?

MSC: Well, the draft year is a tough one for sure, it's going to hit you in some way throughout the next year. It's going to be there, and you're going to think about it, but I think that over this year; watching some players that are involved in the draft, it's definitely something that you can't let affect you. You can't look at all the draft rankings, you can't look at everything that's said about you because some people are going to love you, and some people aren't going to like you too much, so I guess it's kind of funny when one person says you should be going tenth, and the next person says you should be going second or third round. It's just a matter of opinion, and the only person you should be impressing is an NHL team, who will hopefully give you an opportunity in the future.

HP: Yeah, that's true. Ryan Johansen was ranked top 15, some even said he might go top 20—top 25, but he went 4th overall. So you can't always depend on those rankings.

MSC: Definitely

HP: What are you most looking forward to this upcoming season?

MSC: I'm definitely looking forward to getting some wins. Last year was a pretty hard year for the Edmonton Oil Kings, I think we only won about 16 games. It was very tough, especially with the young team, who weren't used to losing that many games. I'm very excited next year to help the up and coming, young team in order to get some wins, because that's what in the end feels awesome! I'm also excited for the draft, I'm not going to let it mess with my head, or take advantage of my on-ice play, but it's definitely something that will help me stretch and be the best I can be, and it's going to push me to be a better player.

HP: You had the opportunity to play for Team West throughout the World Under-17 Hockey Challenge in 2009. What was that experience like and what did you take back from it?

MSC: Anytime you can put on the Hockey Canada jersey, it is an absolutely incredible experience. You never know when you're going to be able to put that jersey on again, and you need to grasp the moment and take advantage of the opportunity you were given. I was fortunate enough to wear the jersey twice; as an under-ager in Port Alberni, and last year in Timmins, Ontario. In both years, we came up a little short, but the feeling you get from putting on the red and white is absolutely incredible. It's definitely a motivator, and I'm definitely looking forward to hopefully wearing it again in the near future.

HP: Where do you draw your inspiration from?

MSC: I think my family; my dad and my brother, who played professional hockey. I also draw it from my grandparents, my sisters, my relatives, my friends, I've always been a little different from most of my friends, school friends at least, who a lot of them have a different life style than me. I want to impress all my friends, I don't want to disappoint, I want to pretty much make the St. Croix name a continuing hockey tradition name.

HP: How would you say you have a different lifestyle than your friends?

MSC: I guess that a hockey life style is a little different than most normal high school kids. You get a curfew a bit earlier and going on the road. It's definitely a different lifestyle, but it's definitely one that is amazing if you're able to do it.

HP: Do you have any words of advice for aspiring Midget or Bantam players out there, dreaming to one day receive the opportunity to play at the higher level?

MSC: Yeah, I'd say just keep on working and do all the extra things. Hockey is a game of details and those little details is what separates a Jonathan Toews or someone who's not up to that level. If you watch Jonathan Toews or an unbelievable player like that, it's all the little details that make him the player that he is. And that is truly what is going to separate you from playing in the NHL, playing in the American league, to not playing professional hockey at all.

HP: You mentioned Jonathan Toews. Does he personally inspire or influence your game?

MSC: For sure, he's from Winnipeg and being from Winnipeg, you have role models, and he's definitely a role model that I can look up to. If you watch him play, he does every single thing well. He can go a game without a point and he would still be one of the best players on the ice. All the little things he does, all the little plays he makes, the compete, the leadership, every part of his game is something that I strive to do. He's definitely my favorite player in the National Hockey League and I'm very proud to say he's from Winnipeg because he's an absolutely incredible hockey player, and has dominated the National Hockey League to this day.

HP: Here's a question to prep you for the combine next year. If you could be an animal—any animal, what would you be and why?

MSC: I'd be a lion because the lion is the king of the jungle. The lion is on top. The lion is proud, but humble. He's going to do whatever it takes to be the leader, to get to the top, and if anyone wants to get to the top, they're going to have to get through him. So, I'd definitely say a lion.

# Matt Puempel
## Left Wing – Peterborough Petes

Matt Puempel could not ask for much more in his rookie season in the OHL. Puempel scored 33 goals and added 31 assists en route to winning the award as the Ontario Hockey League's rookie of the year. Matt was full value for the award and it gives him a great kick start heading into his draft season in 2010/2011.

The Essex Ontario native mixes a blend of scoring and playmaking abilities. Matt showed the ability to adjust to the league quickly and gained the trust of the coaching staff. It's a whole new staff in Peterborough but it should be a safe bet that Puempel will be given plenty of opportunity to play his way into a top draft spot heading into the NHL draft in Minnesota in June of 2011.

# The Interview:

HP: How did your first season with Peterborough go?

MP: It was a lot of fun playing in Peterborough. It wasn't the outcome we were looking at the end of the season in the wins column. But, we came together strong over the year and we thought we should've gone farther. In the end we still got better as the year went on and should continue over the next couple years.

HP: Did you feel much pressure in the beginning of the season after being such a high pick?

MP: Not too much. Peterborough really stressed that they just wanted me to come in and not be a liability on the ice, so that was my goal. I knew if I could do that then the offense would come and it did. I was definitely happy with how things went through the year. I would say no, there was no added pressure.

HP: What was the most difficult part of the transition this past year between Minor Midget and the OHL?

MP: I would say probably the competitiveness and the battles. They are so important at the next level and if you want to survive and win your shift, you need to win every battle to get the puck on your stick. You can't take anything for granted because every player is so good in the league. It's an unbelievable development league and you need to battle each shift and leave it all out there?

HP: Did any of the older guys in Peterborough help out with the transition?

MP: Yeah, for sure definitely. Guys like Therberge and "Breener" (Christopher Breen) were really helpful in the room. "Breener" came over from Erie and was the nicest guy in the world. I got a give a lot to credit to them for helping out. They each have spent a lot of time in the league. Also, Zack Kassian (traded to Windsor) was really helpful because he was from my hometown and showed me the ropes a bit.

HP: What are your strengths on the ice?

MP: I like to think offensively I got a chance to play the power-play this year and it went well so I'm happy with that. Also, just trying to keep it as simple as possible to get the job done. Like I said, not being a defensive liability is important and that was my goal coming into this year and I think I was successful at accomplishing that.

HP: What about some weaknesses?

MP: You know, I want to improve on everything going into next year. It's a big year. Specifically, my skating; being quicker and stronger down low. Hopefully, just keep getting more solid on my skates and not getting knocked down.

HP: What have you been doing to work on these weaknesses?

MP: Well I've been working a lot with my trainer Rob Maggio. I told him what I am looking to do and we've been doing a lot of work with it. I'm trying to get on the ice as much as possible to work on the little things that are tougher to work on when you are in the middle of a season. I want to see a big improvement in my game with off ice conditioning and skating style.

HP: Did you learn a lot about what you need to improve on from your end of the year exit meetings?

MP: Yeah, we had the end of the year meetings and such where the coaches told me what they want me to improve on. But, as I'm sure you know, they are no longer there so I had to identify some things for myself. Obviously, I'm going to do what they suggested as well but I sort of just took a look at how my year went. I am working to improve on that and wait and see what the new coaches have to say.

HP: Where do you think you are most productive on the ice?

MP: I will say in front of the net. I'll do anything to score a goal. I just want to help the team out as much as possible. I know you've got to get to the dirty areas if you want to be good at that. That was a big change coming into the league. There are no easy goals anymore and you have to battle for every single goal.

HP: What has improved most about your game since you joined Peterborough?

MP: You know, probably just learning not to make that extra play. Keeping it simple and then going to work down low. Peterborough really stresses big body hockey and you've got to get down low and win your battles and compete for every part of the ice. I think it was something that we stressed a lot last year and worked out pretty well. Overall, just being down low, being strong, and giving the team a chance to win.

HP: Who are some of the tougher defensemen that you have gone against this season? What about their game makes it so difficult?

MP: Well, I would probably have to go down a list on that one. But, guys like Alex Pietrangelo and the drafted guys. Those guys are really good; the Ryan Ellis' of the league. Pretty much every team has a good top two that you are going to have to face if you have been successful offensively. Each team has two or so guys that you aren't to happy to look at if you are going to have to go up against them.

HP: Do you have any players in the NHL or CHL you like to watch play?

MP: Yeah, I got to go with a couple guys there. My favorite player has always been Jerome Iginla and I know I've been compared to Rick Nash. Anytime you hear stuff like that you have to know they are elite players and you're not going to be ready to be comparable to them, but you need to look at them and watch them play because its special.

HP: If you could pick one player from the 2010 Entry draft that you think your game relates to, who would it be?

MP: Yeah, it's really tough because every player brings an element of their own game that you can improve on personally. Maybe Taylor Hall because we are both from the OHL and I like to think I will do anything to win as well.

HP: When you see how much media attention guys like Seguin and Hall have gotten recently, are you ready to face that as an expected top pick in next years draft?

MP: Yeah, I just think I'm going to take it day by day. Obviously, those are two elite players and to get in that category it requires a lot of hard work over the summer and next year too. They both had unbelievable years to get where they are at and the past couple months with the media stuff. But, yeah, my goal is to be where they are at one day. I need to work hard to make sure I can do that and put myself in a great position.

HP: What is the best piece of advice you have gotten from a coach?

MP: Probably to take nothing for granted. It could all be there one day and nothing the next. You need to keep working hard for your ice time. The OHL is more of a business. Everyone is trying to make a living at it, so you can't take a shift or game off because the next guy in line will take your spot. You need to keep going at it but stay the course if things aren't going away. It is important to recognize you are there for a reason and not to forget that.

HP: What are some of your goals for next season?

MP: It's pretty easy; just do anything I can do to help the team win. If I put that first, I know other good stuff will come. Speaking of Hall, who also does whatever it takes to win and it works as he has won two Memorial Cups. I just want to have that mentality, so that we can play a lot longer next year and not just one round. Our goal is to win the Memorial Cup, and if I just play to win hopefully we can do that and everything else will fall into place.

HP: Have you had any nerves regarding the 2011 Draft?

MP: You know what, like I said earlier, I was there last week and I was nervous and it wasn't even my Draft. There are obviously going to be nerves thinking about what could happen. But, to do what you go to do, you can't think about it when the season starts. This summer you can think about it a bit when you are working out, and after the season you can, but hopefully if I just work hard everything else will fall into place.

HP: What was it like to win the Rookie of the Year award?

MP: That was something really special. It was a goal going into next season, and to look at the names of people who have one that in the past and be recognized by the coaches voting poll. So many great players have won that award. I am so grateful to have won it but it's a recognition of last year and doesn't go any further than that. You got to keep working out because next year people may not remember. But, still, it was really special and I'll never forget it.

HP: Did winning it give you a big confidence boost for next season?

MP: Yeah, I think so. I'm still in a bit of shock about winning it. But, it is a good confidence boost to know I can do this and it means so much to have the confidence that I can handle the play and physicality of the OHL. It'll be good to have that in the back of my mind.

HP: If you could describe yourself as a player to an NHL GM, what would you say?

MP: I like to think just a player that is going to compete every night and do whatever is asked of them to stay in the lineup and on the ice. I will put the team first and know that I am helping myself if the team is doing well. Put the team first and everything else works itself out.

HP: What kind of animal would you be and why?

MP: I might go with the Kangaroo: They are pretty quick, get away from their enemies fast, driving wide to get where they need to be.

# Jordan Binnington
## Goalie – Owen Sound Attack

Jordan Binnington played in 22 games for the Owen Sound Attack as a rookie in 2009/2010. The Richmond Hill Ontario native posted a 6-10 record on a non playoff team with a 4.38 goals against average. Jordan had a couple of rough outings which inflated his numbers a bit. The rookie tender had a rude welcome to the league as the Barrie Colts fired 49 shots his way en route to a 9 goal outburst.

Binnington was selected 40th overall by the Attack as their second pick in the 2nd round of the 2009 OHL draft. Jordan was the 3rd goalie selected behind Tyson Teichmann (Belleville 1st round) and Matt Mahalak (Plymouth 2nd round). Binnington was chosen out of the Vaughan Kings organization. Binnington will battle Scott Stajcer (N.Y Rangers 5th round 2009) for playing time as he tries to impress scouts in his NHL draft season.

# The Interview:

HP: How did you go about choosing to play hockey, and goalie specifically?

JB: When I was younger, playing hockey as my favorite sport. I just tried goalie and liked it so I pursued it.

HP: Did you feel pressure this season at Owen Sound after being a high pick in the OHL Draft?

JB: Well, I try not to worry about that stuff but there is always pressure with everything. I try to block it out as much as I can; but my teammates and family have helped me out a lot in terms of staying calm.

HP: Overall how did the season go for you at Owen Sound?

JB: It was all right. There were definitely some games where I got "lit up" for lack of a better word. It was obviously tough, but it went pretty well. As the season went on I matured a lot. Without those couple of tough games, my season would've looked a lot better on paper.

HP: So what style goalie do you see yourself as?

JB: I would say probably a hybrid goalie. I play up and down. I'm pretty flexible so I can make the desperation saves.

HP: What was the most difficult thing to adjust to in the OHL as a goalie?

JB: For sure the speed of the game. Everything develops a lot faster so you have to improve your reaction time; even as a goalie.
HP: What do you think improved most about your game this season?

JB: I would say without a doubt my mental toughness. I think I have grown a lot in that area as both a goalie and a person.

HP: In terms of mental toughness, say you let up a soft goal; how do you go about bouncing back from that?

JB: Well, in minor hockey I had a problem because I got too angry after stuff like that. I've started not to worry about it though. I try just to get past it and not think about it. That has worked out well for me.

HP: Do you play to make the next save instead of worrying about the most recent one?

JB: Yeah, that's what works.

HP: So, what do you consider as some of your strengths on the ice?

JB: I consider my strengths to include my technique, my flexibility, learning how to read the play better and my position in the crease. I would say I'm also good at playing the puck.

HP: What about some things you want to improve on?

JB: Some things I still want to improve on are my flexibility and my strength. That is one thing I'm working on a lot this summer. You can also never go wrong by working on mental focus.

HP: How do you go about working on "mental focus"?

JB: Well preparation for the games is definitely one. You just want to always be ready to go in that sense.

HP: What are you doing this offseason to work on that?
JB: Yeah, I have a personal trainer who I've been working with since the end of the season. I've been gaining a lot of weight, which is good. I'm definitely getting bigger, stronger and faster.

HP: What is the best piece of advice you have received from a coach?

JB: My goalie coach is always giving me good insight and keeping me motivated. Picking one specific thing is tough. But, the best thing he reminds me of is to keep battling; to do whatever you can to make the save.

HP: What are you goals for the upcoming season?

JB: Obviously to play as well as I can. I have also been setting some goals for myself in terms of lower numbers. I just want to have a strong season.

HP: Have you had any nerves about the 2011 Draft?

JB: No, I'm trying not to worry about it. I'm going to do what I can, work hard and just try not to worry about it.

HP: Who has been the toughest offensive player you've had to go against?

JB: That's another tough one. I'm thinking about the guys that have scored against me. Windsor is a tough team to play against for sure. Also, Nazem Kadri has given me some trouble along with Peter Holland on Guelph.

HP: Do you have any NHL or CHL goalies you like to model your game after?

JB: Yeah, Marc-Andre Fleury is a big one. I've watched him for a couple years now ever since he reached the NHL. I love his technique and how he reads the plays. I like to watch that; and other NHL games just to study the goalies and what they do. I watch him the most though.

# Nathan Beaulieu
## Defense – Saint John Sea Dogs

Nathan Beaulieu is a 6'2" 180 pound defenseman with the Saint John Sea Dogs. Beaulieu is a late 1992 birth (Dec 92) which makes the 2010/2011 season his NHL Draft year.

The rear guard brings offensive tools to the Sea Dogs back end. Last season he put up 12 goals and added 33 assists. Nathan will already have 115 regular season games under his belt before his NHL Draft season even begins. The experience should help him all year long as he progresses towards the June draft in Minnesota.

Beaulieu has all the tools and the smarts to make a big impact this season. He has a solid chance to be a high end draft pick next June.

# The Interview

HP: Can you explain to our readers why you are QMJHL eligible?

NB: When I was fourteen years old I moved to New Brunswick with my family and I was drafted in the QMJHL. My family did move to London recently but since I was drafted over there, I play over there as well.

HP: How did this season go with St. John?

NB: I think it went very well. I'm pretty happy with my season and I am looking forward to next season even more because of it. I obviously want to have a better season as I could be a pick in next year's draft. But, overall last season I think I was successful and I'm hoping for a better one next year.

HP: What were the major differences between this season and last?

NB: I think I was much more prepared for my second season. I think my first season in the Q I realized a lot about what I needed to focus on in my game. I worked on that a ton and fortunately it paid off as we had a nice year.

HP: What was the playoff experience like this season?

NB: It was a great experience. Not many 17 year olds get to go through that so I'm very fortunate that I have so much playoff experience under my belt already. Hopefully I can bring that experience into next season and help us go farther.

HP: What was the difference between playoff and regular season hockey?

NB: Definitely the intensity. During the season you can sometimes get by with not getting everything done in every game.

But, in the playoffs, the intensity makes you so dialed into every game and it comes naturally.

HP: What role do you play with St. John?

NB: I'm an offensive defenseman. I like to contribute on both ends with speed and I play on the power play. I like to jump into the rush and am very offensive, but also like to take care of my own end.

HP: What are some of your strengths on the ice?

NB: I would say my shot and my instincts. I think growing up watching so much hockey has helped. My dad coaching major junior for 16 years is a big help. He has coached me since I was born. I guess just watching so much hockey, reading the play well and knowing how to jump in.

HP: How has your father helped you develop your game?

NB: Well I think it is a huge advantage. My dad knows the game very well and I know I can turn to him if I have a question and get the right answer. Not many other kids get to say that so I definitely use it to my advantage.

HP: What are some things you are trying to improve on?

NB: I would say my skating. You can always be a better skater considering how the game moves so fast. But, in all honesty, every part of my game can improve. I work on every part of my game all the time.

HP: Do you have any players on St. John that you look up to?

NB: Yeah, I would say Alex Grant. He is a draft pick of Pittsburgh and will be playing in the NHL some day. He was an older player and he took me under his wing; he was always really helpful. He told me the do's and don'ts of major junior hockey

HP: What about a player from the NHL?

NB: Yeah, I would have to go with Drew Doughty. I like to model my play after him; playing very offensively but also strong in your own zone. Also, guys like Mike Green and Duncan Keith: players that can contribute on the offensive zone but take care of their end as well.

HP: Have you had any nerves regarding the 2011 Draft?

NB: You know, I was fortunate enough to attend the 2010 Draft. My agent took me just so I can get the experience under my belt. I'm not trying to think about it too much. All I need to do is have a good season and leave the rest to the NHL teams. It's in my hands for now though.

HP: What are your goals for next season?

NB: Hopefully this year I can get a world junior tryout. Also I'd really like to make the CHL Top Prospects game as a way to improve my stock.

HP: What has been the most memorable moment of your hockey career?

NB: I'd probably say playing at the U-17's in British Columbia or last year's playoff run. I love being part of a special team, and you don't get the opportunity that much. So, it is just an unbelievable experience to be part of that.

HP: Which NHL Team is your favorite?

NB: The Washington Capitals.

HP: If you could pick one player on the Caps and take his role next season, who would it be?

NB: Mike Green.

# Nick Shore
## Forward – U of Denver (NCAA)

Nick Shore is familiar with following in his brother's footsteps. Drew Shore is attending the University of Denver after playing for the United States National Team Development Program, something Nick has decided to do as well. With the USNTDP last season, Nick racked up 19 goals in 65 games. He also led Team USA with 38 assists. Like many other Americans eligible for the 2011 draft, Shore has good size at 6-feet, 190 pounds. Known as a scorer, the talented center will take his skills to Denver in 2010-11 and look to develop his game further.

## The Interview

HP: How did you get started with hockey? Were there family or friend influences?

NS: I started at a pretty young age because my older brother was always playing. We both needed something to do and hockey was basically what we chose.

HP: What other sports have you played?

NS: My dad played lacrosse in college, and my brother and I played lacrosse basically until we started playing hockey.

HP: What was it like playing for the USA National Team Development Program?

NS: It was a great experience for me. We went to Ann Arbor and you know, this year we had a lot of success winning the World (Under-18) Championships in Belarus so it was a great experience.

HP: With the USNTDP, you play against United States Hockey League and Division 1 college teams. What transitions did you undergo to adapt to the style of play and maybe a new role on the team from previous years?

NS: Well this was the first year we played in the USHL, so that was a step up from what we played the year before. Most of the big D-1 college games we played were really good for us because it was a chance to play at a higher pace, and it worked out pretty well for us.

HP: What went into the decision making process of choosing to attend the University of Denver? Did your brother have any influence?

NS: Yeah, that had a little draw to me, but also I have a lot of respect for the coaching staff and everything. They've been having a lot of success especially with moving players to the next level. I thought that was just the right fit for me hockey-wise.

HP: What do you bring to the table on and off the ice? Who do you model your game after?

NS: I like to think I'm a good character kid and I work hard. On the ice, I think my strengths are my vision, hockey-sense and my shot. Off the ice, I'm a good student. That's another reason I'm going to college, and I'm looking forward to the whole experience. I wouldn't say there's one player I try to model my game after, but if there's one player I certainly like watching, it's Ryan Getzlaf. He's probably one of the players I emulate my game after.

HP: What are your weaknesses? What things do you need to do to take your game to the next level?

NS: I'm always trying to improve on my skating to become more explosive. You know, I've been working hard on that lately and it keeps improving. I'm always looking to get better at that.

HP: Who are the best players that you've gone up against in your career and why?

NS: Recently I was at the World Junior camp and there were guys there like Kyle Palmieri, so mostly kids that have graduated from the (US National Team) program. We also played against guys like Erik Gudbranson and the Canadian team.

HP: What has been the most memorable moment of your playing career?

NS: I think it's got to be winning the World (Under-18) Championships in Belarus. It's pretty special. You work basically for two years in Ann Arbor for that and it all paid off at the end.

HP: What do you think of the record number (11) of American players selected in the first round of the 2010 draft? Why do you think the United States is producing more talent than ever before?

NS: I think hockey just keeps growing in America. A lot of kids are playing hockey and the programs are doing a great job. The draw to hockey is a lot bigger now, so I hope we can keep it up.

HP: How does it feel to be a potential draft pick of the NHL?

NS: It's definitely really exciting. You know, you try not to worry about it that much and just focus on your hockey. It's definitely something to look forward to after the season.

HP: If you could make a pitch to an NHL team on why they should draft you, what would you say?

NS: I'd say that I'm a reliable two-way center that does all the little things right and fits in pretty much anywhere. I think I can play in all situations.

# Cameron Brace
## Center/RW – Owen Sound

Cameron Brace started last season in Huntsville Ontario playing for the Huntsville Otters in the OJHL. Brace got better and better all year long and that led to the callup with the Attack late in the 2009/2010 season. Brace played well in his limited number of OHL games and got a taste of what to expect in his NHL draft year this season.

The former Toronto Jr. Canadien played his way into the OHL draft with a very strong OHL Cup showing which led to Owen Sound selecting him in the 8th round. That pick looks like a steal based on last season.

Brace will need to bulk up and get stronger as he is not a huge body out on the ice. Brace will showcase his lightning fast speed both with and without the puck to NHL scouts this year.

# The Interview

HP: You played most of this season with Huntsville. How did that go?

CB: It went pretty good I think. In the very beginning, I started off a little bit slow, but when I got used to the level and the pace it started going a lot better and it was a good season, overall.

HP: What was your first taste of OHL action like with Owen Sound?

CB: It was really good. The guys treated me really well. The level of hockey was a lot different, though. It was incredibly fast. Still, it was a really good experience and I think it went well. My call up was towards the end of the year when they got into a bunch of injury trouble.

HP: How did the first game of your OHL career feel?

CB: To be honest, it was a little overwhelming. The hockey was just so much better and faster so it was a big change. So, in that sense it was tough, but it still was really good.

HP: Did any veterans on the Attack help you out with your adjustment?

CB: Yeah, for sure. The captain Marcus Carroll helped me a lot in practice with the defensive zone and breakouts. Also, my linemates Doan and Childerly helped me out a lot.

HP: What role did you play in your small sample with Owen Sound?

CB: Well, as soon as I got there they threw me right into the lineup quickly. I just mostly played on the energy line so I just started playing and working hard. I was passing a lot so more of a playmaker's role.

HP: Was playing on the energy line a new experience for you?

CB: Yeah, it was something new, but it was good to get a change and try something different.

HP: Did you have to alter your game a bit for the role?

CB: Yeah, absolutely. I had to change more of my defensive play and help out a lot more in the defensive zone.

HP: What did you learn about your game in that sample that you need to improve on?

CB: I definitely need to improve in the physical aspect of the game. It is more tough and physical in the OHL. I need to be able to get stronger on the boards.

HP: What was the biggest difference between the OHL and midget play?

CB: I would say the transitions between zones; it all happens a lot quicker. You could be heading one way at full speed and within seconds you have to go right back the other way, so I'd say the transitions. You have a lot less time to make decisions.

HP: What do you consider some of your strengths on the ice?

CB: I would say my speed and my awareness. Also, my passing abilities are pretty good.

HP: Where are you most productive on the ice; such as in transition, in the corners, etc.

CB: I feel like I'm strongest when I'm coming out of our own defensive zone with the puck. I'm able to gather a lot of speed coming out of the zone so I'm able to make some good plays.

HP: Do you have any NHL or CHL players that you like to model your game after?

CB: I don't exactly model my game after anyone. I like the way Matt Lombardi plays because he is fast and a little small. I would say Andrew Cogliano is another.

HP: What about their games do you specifically like to watch.

CB: Well yeah I really try to play like Lombardi but more so Cogliano because I really like the way he moves on the ice and his offensive/defensive awareness. Also the speed that Cogliano carries through the neutral zone really puts defenseman on their heels and then he can make his move.

HP: Who was the toughest defenseman or forward you had to go against the OHL this season?

CB: I feel like the most difficult player I had to play against was checking Kadri. He is really good at slowing down the play and is smart in the offensive zone.

HP: What have you been working on this summer? Does Owen Sound have you doing anything specific?

CB: Yeah, I had an end of the year with all the coaching staff. They just told me I have to keep working hard this summer, gain a little of strength. Just the standard stuff; hitting the gym.

HP: Are you working on this with a trainer, or on your own?

CB: I actually do mostly own thing. They gave me a workout regimen to follow and I've been the best I can with that.

HP: Why not with a trainer?
CB: Yeah, I feel like I work harder and better when I'm pushing myself and responsible for myself.

HP: What's the best piece of advice you've ever received from a coach?

CB: A lot of coaches in the past have told me always just to work hard and keep going, and that really helps. When you keep going it seems to help you play your best.

HP: If you were an animal, what kind of animal would you be?

CB: I would say a lion because I like to be at the top of the food chain.

HP: What are your personal goals for next season?

CB: I want to be a good third or second line centerman. I want to work hard and produce at a higher level than I did in my 15 game sample. I have confidence that I can do that, as well.

HP: What does it take to be a solid #2 or #3 center in the OHL?
CB: Well, number one it takes hard work. You have to work a lot harder, be more physical, and be able to match up against other team's second line centers. I think that's the number one thing I'm excited to work on.

HP: What are you most excited about for this season?

CB: What I'm most excited about for this year is trying to make the team and play a full year. I hope I can get some points and most importantly help the team win.

# Jonathan Huberdeau
## Center– Saint John SeaDogs

The difference between making the NHL and falling into oblivion is often the player's willingness to work hard off the ice. Jonathan Huberdeau, a center for the Saint John Sea Dogs, will have to spend a lot of time bulking up to play professionally. At 6-foot-1, 155 pounds, Huberdeau is extremely slight. However, that has not stopped scouts from raving about his skills. The 17-year-old, 16 during the season, tallied 15 goals and 20 assists in 61 games in his rookie campaign in the QMJHL. He has a good shot and is adept as a set-up man. Huberdeau has plenty of time to get his body ready for the NHL while returning to Saint John in 2010-11.

# The Interview

HP: Jonathan, you had a great rookie season with the Sea Dogs last year. How did it compare going from a Midget AAA francophone environment to a QMJHL Anglophone environment?

JH: Of course it was tougher for the language going there and talking only in English, but it was one of my goals to learn English because it's something very important. For the caliber of the game, I started with the rookies training camp which was mostly my caliber, and then as the veterans came in you had to up your game and I think I was able to adjust well to that.

HP: Talking about the caliber of the play, what was the biggest difference between the QMJHL and Midget AAA?

JH: I would say the skating; I wasn't the fastest on the team. In fact I was probably one of the slowest, but I was able to improve it during the season. Also the physical play is really different; guys are older and stronger than in the other calibers I played in. The ambiance on the ice isn't really the same.

HP: Did playing with two great offensive veterans like Nicholas Petersen and Mike Hoffman help you a lot?

JH: Yeah, we probably had the 3 best 20 years olds in the league. It helps you to see them every day and when you need help they are there to help you. And it helps you break your limits because in order to play with them you have to try to be as good as them. When the coach wanted to reward me, he sent me with them and you saw the difference. At the same time it made me a better player by trying to be as good as them so I can just wish them the best in their careers.

HP: How do you train this summer to be ready for training camp?

JH: I don't think I've changed a whole lot in my training; I'm not stressed with my draft year. I train like I did last year, I put some more emphasis on putting on more weight and working on leg strength but I train once a day like a did last year.

HP: Do you have any objectives for next season?

JH: No, I don't have any objectives. I want to play without pressure. I'll play like I did last year without pressure and it went pretty well.

HP: How did playing the President Cup's final help you progress as a player and what did you learn while playing it?

JH: I learned that it's not because it's the playoffs that you have to change your play. It's like a season but a second one. So the veterans have to relax the young players so they play the same way. We had a meeting before the playoffs to tell us to play without any pressure and I'll try to bring that to the younger players next year. Of course, the play is quicker, but you get used to it as it goes on.

HP: What are your strengths?

JH: I would say my vision on the ice; I see it very well. I'm a complete player. I can play in every situation, powerplay and penalty kill. I can play in an offensive role and a defensive role that's not a problem for me.

HP: What are your weaknesses?

JH: My skating of course, I have to improve it, but you can always improve it. I have to shoot more also, sometimes I am in the slot and I don't shoot, so I have to correct that. But as the season went on and the coaches told me to shoot, I think it started to be better.

HP: What evolved the most in your play this season?

JH: I can't really say because I don't get to see myself play. I practice every day so yeah I've improved many assets of my game, but I think the others would be better to say that than me. I'd say practicing every day and with better players makes you a better player and your execution gets quicker also.

HP: You scored 15 goals at 16 years old which is pretty impressive but you also had a +28 differential. Is this something important for you to be in the plus?

JH: I never told myself I have to be good in the defensive zone, it's just something that came with my vision I think. I can see plays develop in my own zone so I can react because I see them. I like it when the coach tells me to go on the ice for a defensive shift.

HP: To whom would you compare in the NHL?

JH: I would compare myself to Mike Ribeiro... on the ice of course. (Laughs) On the ice a bit, in the shootouts he's a bit like me and my skating, I've been told, looks like him.

HP: Do you compare yourself to a player in the QMJHL?

JH: I don't, but I've been compared to Yannick Riendeau (The 2008-2009 player with most points) of the Drummondville Voltigeurs because he wasn't a very good skater but managed to score a lot of goals and be a very good player.

HP: What has been the best advice you've been given in your hockey career?

JH: My father gave me the best advice I've ever been given. He told me to have fun. Some parents put pressure on their kids when they play hockey but my parents just told me to have fun and never put pressure on me. My father told me if you go to the arena and you don't have fun, tell me and we'll find something else to do than hockey.

HP: What was your relationship like with your coach Gerard Gallant?

JH: It was pretty good. As soon as I arrived he really trusted me. He told me you will play with us, you will play often I won't let you rot up in the stands. Many coaches in the league keep some 16 years olds on the roster and don't let them play often, but he put me on the ice for the important face-offs on the penalty killing and on the power play. So yeah it was pretty motivating and fun for me.

HP: What advice would you give to the younger players who want to play in the QMJHL like you?

JH: Do your best and have fun. That's what I remember doing in my minor hockey and I had a great time.

HP: In your opinion, what does it take to play in the NHL?

JH: I really don't know because I'm not there right now, but I know I can't identify one quality of a player that makes you go to the NHL. I mean every player is different and every team needs different players. You can have a little bit of talent and be on a 4th line in the NHL so I wouldn't say talent is the necessary quality to play in the NHL, I'd rather say desire and work.

HP: You played against the Wildcats in the President Cup, how was it playing against big defensemen like David Savard and Brandon Gormley?

JH: That's where I saw that those guys are very near NHL caliber. They have experience and they always know what they're doing on the ice. It was a lot tougher to play Moncton than to play Gatineau because of these guys. It's tougher to fore-check on these guys than any others in the league.

HP: The last question is from the crazy NHL Combine Test. They ask these questions to the young prospects like yourself so it's a bit weird but do your best to answer it. If you were an animal what would you be?

JH: Oh, that's tough to answer quickly, maybe a Sea Dog? (Laughs) I really don't know... I'd say a Lynx because of his vision and my strength is my vision so I'd say it fits.

(Interview was conducted in French)

# Sean Couturier
## Center – Drummondville Voltigeurs

Sean Couturier might just be the next NHL superstar to come out of the Quebec Major Junior Hockey League. At 6-foot-4, 190 pounds, Couturier has the ideal size and skill to excel at the highest level. With Drummondville last season, he tied for the league lead in scoring with 96 points in just 68 games. Couturier possesses an NHL-ready shot that helped him net 41 goals in 2009-10. He was also an astounding plus-62 last season, showing his responsibility in all areas of the rink. Because of his phenomenal offensive skill-set and elite two-way ability, Couturier could be the top-pick in the 2011 draft

## The Interview

HP: After a season of 31 points as a 16 years old, you had a 96 point season last year. You finished first for the most points in the league. From your point of view, was there a big difference in your play between the two seasons?

SC: In my first season, I had a different role with the big names we had and the fact that I was a rookie, I tried to learn as much as I could from our veterans and from my experience at the Memorial Cup. Then with a good training program during the summer and the participation at the U-18 tournament, it gave me a lot of confidence to enter my 17 year old season.

HP: During your rookie season, you played with two great 20 year old players, Yannick Riendeau and Danny Massé. How did it help you to see those two guys work?

SC: Everything they do is impressive. You look at them every day and you try to be like them. How they prepare for the games, how they focus, their work ethic, they were players that worked hard during the practices.

HP: Tell me your thoughts on your experience at the Memorial Cup and the President Cup in 2009.

SC: At the time, I tried to enjoy it as much as I could because I knew it's something that happens every year. I worked as hard as I could and tried to have fun.

HP: Is it tough for you to motivate yourself for the next season since you finished first in the points department last season?

SC: No, not really. I'll have to prove myself again next season; I'll have a little bit of pressure of course with the season I had last year, but those things are part of hockey. I'll try to work as hard as I can to improve myself and to be ready for training camp.

HP: How do you train this summer to be ready for the next training camp?

SC: I try to put on some weight and improve my skating; those are my two biggest weaknesses. I'll try to be in the best shape possible for training camp.

HP: If you were scout what would you say are your biggest strengths?

SC: I am a good two way player, defensively I'm reliable and even in my offensive play you can see it. I also have really good puck protection skills and I think it is my biggest strength.

HP: What would be your weaknesses?

SC: As I said, my skating is weakness. I am working to improve right now. I want to have more explosion on my first steps to get my speed quicker.

HP: Which NHL player would you compare yourself to?

SC: I would compare myself to Jordan or Eric Staal.

HP: At 16 years old, you had Guy Boucher as coach. Did he help you a lot?

SC: Yes, of course. He's been really good for me. He knew how to use me at 16 years old and I learned a lot of things. It helped me a lot to progress to my 17 year-old year.

HP: And how was your relationship with Mario Duhamel last season?

SC: As a new coach, we needed time to adapt to his coaching but it wasn't really long as he kept the same philosophy that the team had a year before, so it went pretty good.

HP: You had the best plus/minus of the league last season. Is it important for you to be ranked high in this category?

SC: I take it seriously, yes. I think it's really important in hockey if you want to graduate to be good defensively, because if you are not, you won't play the big minutes when the score is tied or you want to keep the lead.

HP: At only 18 years, you are a veteran in this league. How can you help the rookies starting their major junior career with the Drummondville Voltigeurs next season?

SC: The most important thing I'd say is the attitude. You have to keep thinking positively, always work hard and just get to know the guys in the team. To be on our team you need a good work ethic because that's what we base our philosophy on.

HP: In your opinion, what does it take to make it to the NHL?

SC: Of course, you have to be good offensively, but I think it's more important to be good defensively. I'm going to try to get better at it because you need to be able to play those big minutes in the NHL because whenever you are on the ice in the NHL, it's big minutes.

HP: What's been the best advice anybody ever gave you regarding your hockey career?

SC: I think it's just to have fun to playing hockey. If you don't have fun playing hockey it's not going to work. It's by working hard that you are going to get results and eventually have more fun.

HP: Do you feel some pressure coming into the next season as the top prospect for the next NHL Entry Draft?

SC: Of course, people talk about it, but I don't put myself under pressure before the season. Maybe when the season will begin it'll be different, but as of now I try to approach the season the same way as I did at 16 and 17 years old.

HP: What are the assets in your play that improved the most since you entered the QMJHL.

SC: I would say my skating improved a lot and my work ethic that I learned with Guy Boucher in my first year.

HP: Are there any players in the QMJHL that helped you personally or professionally in your career?

SC: I would not say a player; I'd rather say my father who has always followed me in the arenas everywhere I played. The fact that he's always been involved in some way in the hockey world helped me because I've always been in it and it kept my interest in hockey.

HP: Now it's time for the crazy NHL Combine Test question. If you were an animal, what would it be and why?

SC: Hmmm, I would be a bull I think because it's tough to get him off balance, It's really big physically and strong and that's what I would compare my style to.

*(Interview was conducted in French)

# Brandon Saad
## LW/RW – Saginaw Spirit

At 6-foot-2, 196 pounds, Brandon Saad has NHL-ready size at just 17. The skilled winger ruled the North American Hockey League in 2008-09 with 29 goals and 18 assists in 47 games. Saad entered the United States National Team Development Program in 2009-10 and excelled right away. He buried 29 goals and 29 assists in 63 games. With his size, skill and character, Saad will likely be a high first-round pick in this year's NHL Draft. A first-round pick in the Ontario Hockey League Draft in 2008, Saad will play for the Saginaw Spirit in 2010-11.

## The Interview

HP: How did you get started with hockey?

BS: I actually started skating when I was two. My cousins played and my mom took me and my brother to the local rink. I just fell in love with the game and stuck with it.

HP: What other sports have you played?

BS: I played all the sports growing up like baseball, soccer, football, everything but basketball pretty much. I played that with my friends and stuff but never on a team.

HP: What was it like playing for the USA National Team Development Program?

BS: It was a lot of fun and a good experience, especially winning gold with the U-18 team. It was an unbelievable experience, and it was a great program.

HP: With the USANTDP, you play against United States Hockey League and Division-1 college teams. What transitions did you undergo to adapt to the style of play and maybe a new role on the team from previous years?

BS: We played against tougher competition and older guys. It was definitely a change to step up your game and work harder, but all in all, hockey is hockey, and you just have to play harder and work harder to bring your game up to another level.

HP: Why did you choose to go the OHL route and play for the Saginaw Spirit this season? How do you think it will help in your development?

BS: They went back and forth with me and my family. Next year I'm going to be a senior in high school, so instead of looking at the USHL and then to college, we decided I'd play more games in the OHL and elevate my game and hopefully make it to the NHL one day. I think it should help a lot. We'll be a pretty good team next year, and it's a great league. I'll be playing in a good atmosphere.

HP: How different has the preparation and training been so far in the OHL?

BS: There was a big difference in training last year with the national team. You just have to stick with those habits and work hard on and off the ice. Knowing it's a tougher league, you just have to step up your game and work harder.

HP: What do you bring to the table on and off the ice? Who do you model your game after?

BS: I think I'm a leader and can step up in big games and work hard. I lead by example on and off the ice by staying out of trouble and just working hard in the weight room, that kind of stuff. When Jaromir Jagr used to be in the NHL, I think I play similar to him a little bit. I'm not quite sure exactly who I play like in the NHL, but I know guys I watch are Sidney Crosby and Malkin are both good role models.

HP: What are your weaknesses? What things do you need to do to take your game to the next level?

BS: I think there's not one thing that I'm real weak at, but there's nothing that I can stop working at for sure. All the little things are important you know. There's never one thing you can stop working at.

HP: Who are the best players that you've gone up against in your career?

BS: Probably all the competition against college players. Overseas is tough too, but I think playing against colleges with some older guys that are bigger is really tough.

HP: What has been the most memorable moment of your playing career?

BS: I think definitely winning the gold medal in Belarus with the U-18 national team was the best memory.

HP: What do you think of the record number (11) of American players selected in the first round of the 2010 draft? Why do you think the United States is producing more talent than ever before?

BS: I think every year you see Americans like this year getting drafted. It gets people to start watching the game more. I think just seeing that other people can do it gets people involved.

HP: How does it feel to be rated as a potential first-round pick in the NHL Draft?

BS: It's definitely a big honor but nothing that I'd look too much into. I still have to work hard and play my game. Whatever happens, happens.

HP: If you could make a pitch to an NHL team on why they should draft you, what would you say?

BS: I'd say that I do the little things and also whatever it takes to win. No matter what is asked, I'd do it just to win. With my playmaking ability, I can help a team out a lot. Also, the penalty kill or power play, really anything they need me for I'll work on.

# Patrick Koudys
## Defense – RPI

With the NHL game becoming faster, the need for big, shutdown defenseman has increased to combat the level of skill. Players like Zdeno Chara and Chris Pronger are coveted due to their size and strength. Patrick Koudys, a blueliner headed to RPI this season, is looking to become one of these valuable assets. At 6-foot-4, 195 pounds, Koudys uses his size to muscle opponents off the puck. His defensive play is his best trait, but he has shown some offensive flair as well. He registered five goals and 28 assists last season with Burlington of the Ontario Junior Hockey League. With a tougher training regimen in college, Koudys will only add size and strength to an already impressive frame.

# The Interview

HP: How did your year go with Burlington of the CCHL?

PK: It was a really good season. We had a really good team this year. We had a great coach this year. One thing I noticed about the team this year is we were the closest team I've experienced. We all got along really well and there were never any disputes between guys so we were able to come together as a team, play hard, and do what we had to do. Like I said, Mark Juris was great for us and me personally. We had a pretty good stretch in the playoffs, but I wish we could've made it through. For me, I was really happy with how my season went.

HP: For how long have you had a desire to play NCAA Hockey?

PK: Well, my uncle used to play for RPI, so I guess it has always been in the family that way. I guess growing up I didn't think about it much because I just wanted to keep playing hockey as long as I could. I hadn't really thought about how to do that. But, as I got older I thought about what would be the best way to lengthen my career either by eventually getting paid to play the game or stay involved in some other way. I know most kids up here are deciding between the "O" and school so I just weighed the pros and cons. For me, it was a no brainer that school would lengthen my career the most. It would give me the best chance to further my career beyond school as well. Also, I like the idea of getting an education from such a great school like RPI. I would say that around the time of my OHL draft year is when I really started to decide that I wanted to play college hockey.

HP: RPI is a smaller school but known for a great hockey program. Did you receive much attention from some of the bigger name schools that made the decision difficult?

PK: Yeah, there were other schools out watching and that is when I really sat down and asked myself what are the top things I wanted in a school. I think I had five things. RPI also offered me a scholarship early, which was a big thing. However, I also wanted to do engineering. RPI has a great program. I love the RPI hockey program and think the coaching staff is top notch. Another was being close to home, and RPI is only about five hours or so from my home. I think at RPI I will be able to step in and contribute to a winning team early in my career. There are obviously other small factors, but those were the big ones. I definitely compared RPI to some of the bigger name schools, but it just seemed RPI was the best fit for me by far. No matter what school offered me anything, I think RPI would be the best fit. It was a no brainer.

HP: Many players that go the NCAA route do so they can go on a heavy workout program to add size? Was that part of your decision process?

PK: Yeah, that was definitely part of it. I guess when you are comparing major junior to the NCAA, there are a lot less games in college hockey. I think that means in NCAA hockey, you get a lot more training, which I think is more beneficial. You are on the ice during the week; you are practicing more and training more, which I thinks puts you at a physical advantage. Also, on a game day you can hope for 10-15 minutes in a game. In a practice you are on the puck for 2 hours or so. For me, NCAA hockey, in that sense, with the training and practice, you do tend to get a lot stronger and better. I would say that is going to help me lengthen my career and hopefully become a pro.

HP: What role do you think you play on the ice?

PK: Well, I've never thought of myself as being in a specific role. Coaches in the past have told me I'm a two way player that can play in the offensive or defensive zone. I guess I see myself as a player that will play any position or role the coach wants. I think my defensive play is my best asset, but I can contribute offensively as well. Lately, my offensive game has improved a lot, so I think a two way player is a good position for me.

HP: What about some things you are trying to improve?

PK: You know, I'm just trying to improve my whole game. I'm happy with how I'm playing right now, my physical ability and where I'm at right now. But, I'm excited to just get to school, get in the gym, train with the guys and see how they do it at the next level. On the ice, I want to get used to their speed, and just learn from older, more experienced players. I want to pick up some of the tricks and improve everything. I think about how Sidney Crosby still tries to improve every aspect of his game, so I should have the same goal. I guess getting as strong, fast, and skilled as I can is the goal.

HP: What do you envision your role to be next year with RPI?

PK: I'm a young guy coming in; a true freshman at 18 years old. I think I'll be the youngest on the team. I think in that sense it will be tough and a challenge but I'm really looking forward to it. Coach has said I should have a good shot to play and put minutes on the board, but it will require work. Like I said, I'll do whatever coach wants me to do for him; whether it is the power play, penalty kill, even strength or anything. Obviously, expectation-wise, anyone would love to be the #1 guy. I just want to be able to rise up the depth chart and do the best I can while working my way up and helping the team win.

HP: Have you thought at all about the 2011 NHL Draft?

PK: There has been some nice, positive talk regarding the draft. I played with Team Canada selects in a three-nation tournament against the Finns and Swedes. There were lots of NHL scouts out there watching. I got a lot of positive feedback from that as well as some teams watching throughout last season. It has been nice because you always want to hope for the best, so it's nice to hear that teams are watching and liking what they see. However, I can't take it too seriously as I need to work to make sure I can get drafted or get drafted high. This year is going to have to be a big year in terms of working hard. I'm actually going to a mini combine up in Toronto with the top 9 prospects from the 2011 draft from every league (OHL, WHL,

QMJHL and NCAA) . I was invited to that which was a huge honor.

HP: Are there any NHL players you like to watch play? What about any former NCAA players?

PK: You know, that's really tough. My coach this year told me that I should watch Zdeno Chara. Obviously, that's a huge compliment. I guess a Chara type player would be a good example because he is a big defenseman that will play any role, from being physical to the power play or penalty kill. Also, I watched some Buffalo games this year and I really enjoyed watching Tyler Myers play. I think he is someone worth molding my game after as well.

HP: What is the biggest challenge you've ever had to overcome in your hockey career? How did you go about overcoming it?

PK: It's hard to label one challenge. I've been very fortunate to be injury free and stuff, but I've certainly had to work hard for everything I've earned or gotten.

HP: What is the best piece of advice a coach has given you?

PK: I'd say every coach I've had has been great for me in terms of passing along little tidbits that are really helpful. It would be hard to label one, but definitely working hard is up there. Mark also told me to play with confidence, which would help me a lot. Another is that you have to earn every minute of your ice time.

HP:  What are you most excited for at RPI?

PK: Well there are a ton of things I'm excited for. I think number one would be that my cousin plays for Bentley University and our home opener is against them. I think that'll be really exciting playing against him and having it be against my cousin. I think the other would be just to get in there with the guys and training. There is nothing better than that. Finally, there is always the hockey part of trying to win a championship, and putting in the work to try and do it.

# Scott Mayfield
## Defense – Youngstown Phantoms

Defensemen usually take longer to develop than forwards, but occasionally a youngster comes along that plays beyond his years. Such is the case with Scott Mayfield, a defender for the Youngstown Phantoms in the United States Hockey League. Mayfield possesses ideal size at 6-foot-3 and has time to grow into his thin 175-pound frame. Despite his skinny stature, Mayfield plays an impressive physical game and is not afraid to mix it up. He is one of the best defenseman from the United States eligible for the 2011 draft because of his incredible instincts and natural ability. He looks comfortable in all areas of the rink. With a booming shot from the point, Mayfield racked up 10 goals and 12 assists for the Phantoms last season and returns to Youngstown in 2010-11. He will be off to the University of Denver in 2011-12 where he will join another potential first-round draft choice in Nick Shore.

# The Interview

HP: How did you go about choosing to play defense?

SM: When I was growing up I was actually a centerman, but then as I grew up and was getting bigger I started moving back more. I was a lot bigger than everyone else so that's probably why I made the move to defense.

HP: Did you have any family influences in terms of choosing hockey?

SM: My mom always wanted my younger sister, my older brother and I to skate. We all started skating at the same time. My brother is three years older than me but I was skating around him. So, we decided I should try on some hockey skates and start playing hockey.

HP: How was your season in Youngstown?

SM: It was an up and down season. We started out doing good. We were around .500 but then we started struggling a bit and went on something like a 12 game losing streak. We had a coaching change. It was just a few up and downs. Personally, it was a great season. It was a great year. We were second to last in the league but I got a ton of playing time, some power play time, and it turned into a productive season.

HP: What is the biggest difference about the USHL?

SM: Well I came straight from U-16 AAA so I didn't go through U-18 AAA or NAHL. So, I would say the speed was the biggest thing. There were bigger guys that made it tough. Moving away from home had an impact because it was my first time.

HP: What role did you play for your Youngstown?

SM: I came in probably as a 5th or 6th, but right away, I moved up to the top pairing. I started over half the games by the end of the season. So, yeah I became a top two Defensman and I was also on the first power play and first penalty kill.

HP: What do you consider some of your strengths on the ice?
SM: I'm very offensive minded. I like to jump through the neutral zone and set up plays in the offensive zone.

HP: A lot of offensive minded defenseman tend to be smaller, but you have a lot of size. Do you think that helps?

SM: I definitely think that helps. Moving the puck up the neutral zone you are going to get hit and bumped so to have my size really helps.

HP: You racked up a lot of PIM's for a player with high offensive numbers. Do you like to drop the gloves every once in a while?

SM: I will fight. I don't really turn them down. That said, I had a lot of plays clearing house in the front of the net. The USHL is a pretty defensive league and you don't get away with as much so I got a lot of penalties in the corners and in front of the net. They were a lot of hitting penalties though, not lazy stuff. I also had four ten minutes from scrums and stuff. They are definitely from an aggressive style of play.

HP: What was your experience like at the research and development camp?

SM: It was great. I was really honored to be chosen for that because all those Canadian kids get a chance to play in the top prospects game. Me and other American kids aren't going to get that. It was great to play at that level. It was the fastest I've ever played in.

HP: Were there any rules they tried out there that you particularly liked?

SM: The USHL plays hybrid icing so I was used to that, and I also like what they were trying with the delayed penalties.

HP: Do you have a player in the NHL you like to watch play?

SM: Well, when I started playing D, Chris Pronger was playing in St. Louis so that's probably the biggest one.

HP: If you're a St. Louis fan, what about Erik Johnson?

SM: That's actually funny. He is my favorite player. He's had some injuries and I was out there skating with him a couple times while he was recovering.

HP: Did he have any useful tidbits for you?

SM: Yeah, when I practiced with him, he had Al Macinnis out there coaching and we did all sorts of drills and stuff. I really liked watching him in the Olympics as well; he was something to watch.

HP: What have you been working on this summer?

SM: Gaining weight. At the end of the season, I was 6'3 and a half and maybe 185 pounds. Now I'm up to almost 200, 197 to be exact. I need to gain weight without losing speed and quickness.

HP: Have you thought at all about the NHL Draft?

SM: I've had some thoughts about what it would be like. I was watching this year and I knew a lot of the players, so it was really cool to see that. I'm not giving it too much thought though; I'm just going out and playing.

HP: So, you are still committed to Denver, is that correct?

SM: I am going to Denver for sure. The only way something would change is if I was a high draft pick and teams had their demands. I gave thought to it this year, but I'm definitely going to play in the USHL this season then head to Denver.

HP: How did you go about choosing Denver?

SM: Well, first of all, my dad went there. He didn't play hockey but he went to law school and has a ton of friends in the area. When I was playing AA hockey and stuff I'd go out there and see the rink and campus. Then at Christmas, when I was younger I got a jersey and that's been hanging above my bed since.

HP: What has been the most memorable moment of your hockey career so far?

SM: Definitely playing overseas for Team USA for the Ivan Hlinka. It felt great to put on the jersey because I never got invited to the NDTP or the national team. So it was great to get the chance to go play.

HP: If you were an animal what kind would you be and why?

SM: I would definitely be a dog because I could live with a family and I'd like to play around all day and not worry about stuff.

# Klarc Wilson
## RW – Edmonton Oil Kings

Klarc Wilson came to the Edmonton Oil Kings last season in trade a that sent forward Brent Raedeke to the Brandon Wheat Kings. Raedeke got an automatic chance to play in the Memorial Cup, while Wilson played for an Oil Kings team that struggled to a 16-win season.

In 33 games with the Oil Kings, the 6'0" 209 pound power forward scored three goals and 13 points.

After a slow start with the Oil Kings, the Edmonton native caught fire down the stretch and really started to find his stride offensively.
After being taken in the first round of the 2008 WHL bantam draft, Wilson is maturing into a proto-typical power forward at the WHL level.

This year, Wilson will play a big role offensively with the Oil Kings and he, along with many of the Oil Kings young corps look to take a big leap forward.

## The Interview

HP: So far in training camp, I'm seeing a much more confident Klarc Wilson out on the ice, who likes to take over the game offensively with your size down low and around the net.

KW: This year is a big year for me. I've got the draft coming up, and I spent the summer training really hard and there are high expectations of me from my coaching staff and my agent and my family. It's my second year and I feel more confident with the puck. If I make a mistake, I just shake it off, and I don't get down on myself like I did last year. I feel like I'm making more plays, I battle hard down low, and everything seems to be working out so far.

HP: Can you talk about the adjustment coming here last year from a team like Brandon who went all the way to the Memorial Cup last year?

KW: It was bittersweet moment. I left a team that had a guaranteed shot at winning a Memorial Cup. It was nice to be a part of it, even though I didn't get a huge opportunity to be a part of their success. Coming here, I got a chance to come home and play on a younger team and getting more of an opportunity to play and be a part of an organization that is rebuilding from the beginning again. We're surrounded by a lot of young players who love to play the game, and in a few years, we're going to be a very competitive team.

HP: You seem more confident this year and you're a lot stronger on the puck. Your overall game has taken a step forward. Right now, what do you feel are your biggest strengths?

KW: I'm a big strong guy and I like being the first guy on the puck in the corners. I use my strength and my size to my advantage. I try to use my vision on the ice and I love to pass the puck. I try to be a force, I try to do a little bit of everything and I can fight if need be.

HP: What are some things that you feel you need to work on heading into your second WHL campaign?

KW: My defensive game and trying to be in position all the time. Last year I had mental lapses where I would make the little mistakes and that's something I need to eliminate from my game. Whether it's going over extensive video, I want to work on the little things and eliminate those small mistakes that can be costly in a game.

HP: Off the ice, what are some of your goals this year?

KW: It's funny you say that… The coaching staff has been weighing me on and off randomly the last three days and the first day I was 209, then yesterday I was 210, and then today I was 208. I seem to be all over the scales. Coach (Derek) Laxdal approached me and said that if I want to be the player he wants me to be, I need to be around the 200 pound mark. Off the ice, I'll be doing a lot of extra bike rides and watching what I eat. I agree with him. I feel like I can be in better shape and be faster, and I'm willing to do whatever it takes to be a more effective player.

HP: Is the draft a big goal of yours?

KW: I want to go as high as possible and work my ass off. Hopefully I hear my name called. Hopefully it's early, but if it's late, that doesn't matter, I just want to get drafted.

HP: When I see you play, I see power forward written all over you? Down the road how do you see yourself filling out?

KW: The coaching staff wants me to play that power forward role, and to be a leader offensively and be a physical player. That's my focus. I feel like I can be a player that the coaches want me to be.

HP: When you look at the team this year, this team is young. You have one player that's been drafted (defenseman Mark Pysyk taken in the first round 23rd overall in 2010) but there's a good crop of players entering your draft year. Are there things that you can draw from a player like Mark Pysyk?

KW: It's something that we can draw on together and we can all learn from this experience. We're fortunate enough to have a first rounder on our team in Mark Pysyk, and we can draw a lot from him. He's the type of guy that you can approach and help you prepare for that kind of stuff. He can joke around with the guys, but he can also be serious, and he's a great guy to learn from.

HP: You talk about being back home and playing in front of your friends and family. Sometimes players can struggle playing in front of your hometown crowd and in front of friends and family. How have you dealt with it?

KW: If anything, it drives me more to be able to play in front of my friends and family. I want to impress them and work hard for them. If I have family that hasn't seen me in a long time, I want to show them how much better I've gotten. They've been a huge part of my hockey success and now I've been given a chance to play in front of them in a very important time in my hockey career. At the start of last year, I was pretty nervous, but now it's my second year, I just want to take a step forward and show them that I'm improving too.

HP: Is there an area of your game where you feel that you're underrated ?

KW: I didn't do as well offensively as I wanted to do. It was a big step moving up from Midget AAA to the WHL. Going through a whole year as 16-year old in the WHL not being able to play every game was a big learning experience. I think people are going to see more offense out of me and I'm going to work hard to get that chance. I'm going to strive to be that more offensive player. Ultimately, I want to be a guy that can be relied on to do a little bit of everything. I feel like I can be a five tool player who can score, set-up goals, fight, and do all the little things to be successful.

# Adam Lowry
## LW – Swift Current Broncos

Adam Lowry was drafted 4th round (78th overall) by the Swift Current Broncos at the 2008 Bantam Draft after coming off a strong Bantam year in the AMBHL, where he led his team to the championship game. Lowry enjoyed a productive rookie season with the Broncos while also doing great in the classroom. For his efforts he was awarded the WHL Scholastic Player of the Year.

Lowry posted 34 points (15 goals, 19 assists) throughout his rookie season with the Broncos. He has also played for Team Pacific at the World U17 Hockey Challenge, and won the WHL Scholastic Player of the Year award for his academic and athletic success.

# The Interview

HP: You just came off your rookie season, where you did very well; you put up a lot of points, you looked good on the ice, and you impressed many people. Any thoughts on the year?

AL: Just going into Swift Current at the beginning of the year, my main goal was to make the team, and just try to improve my situation throughout the year. I knew I'd be starting on the fourth line and [Mark Lamb] told me, "keep working hard, you'll get your opportunity." Then probably ten games into the season, we had a couple of guys out of the line up and I got an opportunity to play on the powerplay. I got a couple of goals and took advantage of the opportunity of more ice time, it just kind of took off from there. I got to play with a lot of really skilled players this year and that really helped me out. We've got a lot of great leaders that just made my first rookie year in the WHL that much more meaningful coming into the next season.

HP: Tell us about getting started playing hockey?

AL: I actually got started playing hockey when I was probably four years old, living in Florida. Hockey's not a big sport down there, and my dad was playing for the Panthers. Then we moved to San Jose. I really started to get my development going in Calgary. I was 8 years old when I came here and I just began moving up the minor hockey ranks in Calgary. Then finally in Bantam they integrated into the Alberta Major Bantam Hockey League, which is one of the better leagues in Western Canada, and that really helped my development. Especially since our team was pretty good. We lost in the finals to Sherwood Park. They have some pretty good players: Reece Scarlett, a teammate of mine, Duncan Siemens and Dylan Busenius. Those were their first three Bantam picks in the Bantam Draft. So we ended up getting swept by them, but playing in Calgary really helped me out.

HP: Were you born in Florida?

AL: I was born in St. Louis, but only lived there for 11 months. Then my dad got traded to Florida and then I lived there until I was 6.

HP: Oh really? Where else have you been?

AL: Well, although I was born in St. Louis, I never really got to experience it. We later moved and I grew up in Florida, but then we moved when I was like 5 years old to San Jose. That's really where I started playing hockey full-time at initiation and tykes levels. Then I moved to Calgary when I was about 8 years old and I've been there ever since.

HP: So, where would you consider home?

AL: Calgary, I'd call Calgary my home.

HP: Would you say you're Canadian or American?

AL: I'd consider myself a Canadian.

HP: So, was it hard adapting to the Western Hockey League?

AL: I don't think it was hard adapting to the Western Hockey League, it just took a little bit of time. This is obviously one of the premier leagues in the Canadian Hockey League, being one of the three. Definitely the speed of the play is not something you're going to get in Midget hockey, no matter where you're playing. It's definitely going to take a little while adapting to the speed, you're going to have to think that much quicker, you're going to have to make those passes half a second earlier and guys are going to be on you. Strength and size is also a factor. Guys are going to be a lot bigger than they were in Midget, and that really was the difference. You have to adapt to guys pushing you off the puck more, you have to learn to work hard to stay with the puck, and you have to battle that much more.

HP: What did the chance to play for Team Pacific at the World U17 Hockey Challenge mean to you and what did you take back from that experience?

AL: That was a huge honor, just because there are so many good forwards coming out of Alberta. To be considered one of the top ones in Alberta is huge. Then when I got there, I got to play with a lot of World Class players. I got to play with Ty Rattie, Mark McNeill, Ryan Nugent-Hopkins, and it just taught me a lot. Our team finished fifth. We were expected to challenge for the title, but it's just so hard to come together in a short competition like that. You just have to realize that everyone's there for the same goal. It's just the experience that lasts a life time, the ability to play with some of those players, they taught me so much. Hopkins is such a great passer, and Rattie is such a good goal scorer. Just watching them and how they prepare before every game, it really helped out. Then there's also a lot of great leadership. Our coaching staff really implemented a system that I can take back and really help my game.

HP: What did you feel you brought to Team Pacific?

AL: I think I brought more of the size and grit than anything. I can put the puck in the net if I'm asked to, but I really felt that I just made space for Hopkins and Rattie, and other players on my line. I'd finish every check, I'd go battle and work hard in the corner, get the puck back for them and let them do what they need to do to be successful.

HP: In contrast to that, what do you feel you bring to the Swift Current Broncos?

AL: I just feel that I'm not necessarily the most skilled or fastest player out there, but I just play the game pretty well and I'm just able to anticipate things that are going to happen, I'm pretty smart with the puck, and I try to make my linemates better.

HP: What parts of your game are you looking to improve on?

AL: Definitely my skating. That's always been a knock against me. My skating needs to improve the most if I'm going to try to take my game to the next level. I've grown a lot over the last few years, so I definitely think that my skating has improved as I've gotten bigger. I just work on it every day at practice, work on my first three strides, just trying to get stronger, trying to get that power so I can keep up with the better skaters in the league.

HP: Who are some guys around the league that have gained a lot of respect?

AL: There are guys like Jordan Eberle. I played against him a lot last year and I have a lot of respect for him. He's one of the best players in the CHL. Then Brandon Kozun, he definitely makes the plays happen every time he's on the ice. If you don't pay attention to him one shift, he'll go out there and score a big goal on that shift. There are also a lot of guys my age like Ryan Nugent-Hopkins, he's put up over 60 points in his rookie season, and plays over thirty minutes a game - that's just amazing. My teammate Reece Scarlett, he's a defenseman and just playing the number of minutes he did, and playing them well like he did. I just have so much respect for him because of the way he plays the game every day.

HP: Who are some of the best chirpers out there? Guys that really get under your skin?

AL: [laughs] well, Saskatoon's full of them. I'd have to say Charles Inglis is pretty good at that. He tries to get in your face and he's pretty effective with it. Darian Dziurzynski and some of his line mates as well. There's a few on the Brandon Wheat Kings; Micheal Ferland is pretty good at getting under your skin and jabbing at you.

HP: You were named Scholastic Player of the Year in the Western Hockey League. Any thoughts on that?

AL: It was definitely a huge honor. Just being recognized for your academic achievements is pretty awesome, but just being at the awards ceremony in general, I got to see a lot of the great players I looked up to like Jordan Eberle and Brandon Kozun. It was all really great and I was really pleased to win that award.

HP: Okay Adam, let's pretend I'm an NHL GM and I ask you, "Adam, tell me why I should draft you."

AL: I'll do whatever it takes to win. I'm pretty big, I'm physical, I can put the puck in the net. I'll do what's asked of me, I'll block a shot, I'll take a puck in the face, I'll draw a penalty. I won't complain if I'm playing four or five minutes, but if I'm playing on the second or third line I'll be happy. As long as the team's winning, I'm happy. I'm a hard worker and I'm a really dedicated guy.

HP: Let's finish up with a silly Combine question; If you were a vegetable in a salad bowl, how would you and the other vegetables escape the bowl?

AL: [laughs] I'd just hope I'm not a vegetable because I don't like salad.

# Seth Ambroz
## RW – Omaha Lancers

Omaha Lancers winger Seth Ambroz is a power forward in every sense. At 6-foot-3 and 198 pounds, the Minnesota native uses his size and strength to dominate opponents. In two seasons in the United States Hockey League, Ambroz has recorded 36 goals and 44 assists. The 17-year-old forward will likely be a high first-rounder in the 2011 draft because of his NHL-caliber size and skill. Ambroz is a well-rounded player with no glaring weaknesses. He will return to Omaha this season and eventually make his way to the University of Minnesota in 2011-12.

## The Interview

HP: How did you get started with hockey? Were there family or friend influences?

SA: Growing up, my brother just kind of got started, and I basically wanted to do what he did and follow in his footsteps.

HP: What other sports have you played?

SA: I played baseball and football until high school. I stopped playing football then, but I still play some baseball.

HP: How does it feel to play for Omaha in the United States Hockey League alongside NHL draft picks?

SA: It feels good. It's a competitive league and a lot of fun. It's a ton of fun to play against the high-caliber players.

HP: What challenges did you face in adjusting to the USHL from high school? What transitions have you undergone to adapt to the style of play and maybe a new role on the team?

SA: It's a lot faster pace and more physical. There's more depth with the teams, but you get used to it. It becomes an everyday thing.

HP: What do you bring to the table on and off the ice? Who do you model your game after?

SA: I bring a big, power forward presence. I like to muck it up in front of the net and in the corners. I'm a physical player for sure. I think a player like Milan Lucic or Dustin Byfuglien type power forward fits my style.

HP: What are your weaknesses? What things do you need to do to take your game to the next level?

SA: I have to work on my first three strides. I need to get quicker. Everything in your game can always be improved, but my quickness is an issue right now.

HP: Who are the best players that you've gone up against in your career and why?

SA: There are many players. I played with Louis Leblanc, and he's a great player. I also played against Jaden Schwartz who was a first-round draft pick last year. There are too many to remember.

HP: What has been the most memorable moment of your playing career?

SA: There are a lot of them. I think playing as a 15-year-old in the USHL was great. There probably isn't one moment in particular.

HP: What are your goals for the upcoming season?

SA: I want to have a great year obviously. I want to be productive and hopefully lead our team to a Clark Cup championship.

HP: How do you think attending the University of Minnesota in 2011-12 will benefit your development?

SA: It's a great program. It always has been. There will be great training and a high competitive level playing in the WCHA. It will be a challenge that way too.

HP: What do you think of the record number (11) of American players selected in the first round of the 2010 draft? Why do you think the United States is producing more talent than ever before?

SA: I think it's great. It shows that America is coming along with hockey as a big-time sport. There are a lot of great players. The U.S. is getting more focused on hockey and that's obviously a good thing.

HP: How does it feel to be rated as a potential first-round pick in the NHL Draft?

SA: It's a great honor. I'm lucky enough to be up there. I just have to work hard from here and hopefully things work out well for me.

HP: Have any of your friends that have been drafted given you any advice?

SA: Not really. They get drafted and just kind of go about their everyday routine. They keep working hard to get to the next level which is what I have to do too.

HP: If you could make a pitch to an NHL team on why they should draft you, what would you say?

SA: I'd be a good presence to have in front of the net and down low. I work really hard,

# Mark McNeill
## Center – Prince Albert Raiders

Mark McNeill was drafted 5th overall by the Prince Albert Raiders in the 2008 Bantam Draft.
The Edmonton native debuted in the WHL in the season following the Draft, where he suited up for the Raiders for four games. Mark suffered a severed Achilles tendon that summer, which hindered his development throughout the summer. The following season McNeill contributed 9 goals and 15 assists, totaling up to 24 points in 68 games as a Raider.

Mark has also played for Team Pacific at the U17 World Hockey Challenge in 2009, and was invited to Team Canada's U18 training camp this summer. A capable and healthy McNeill can be predicted as successful throughout his draft season.

# The Interview

HP: You recently completed your first season in the Western Hockey League. Any thoughts on your season?

MM: I felt it went pretty well. I was facing an injury last spring that put me out through the summer. I was out with a severed Achilles tendon and just coming back from that injury, and getting my speed back to the WHL level and all of that, I felt that I had a pretty good season.

HP: You had the surgery in May. How did that impact your training and upcoming season?

MM: I feel it might've slowed me down throughout summer training because it hinders you in your development, but I felt that by September, I was up and going, had my speed back, and had my game back.

HP: You played for Team Pacific at the U-17 World Hockey Challenge last year, what did the opportunity mean to you and what did you take back from it?

MM: It was great. I love playing against international competition. It's a good experience playing against the other best players my age from around the world. The chance I had to wear my first Canadian sweater was also pretty neat.

HP: How has the Prince Albert Raiders organization helped you develop your game?

MM: They've been great. The coaches, Bruno Campese, Steven Young, and Craig Bedard, they've all been great, working with me after practice and developing all the little things I have to work on. Even when I had my injury they helped me battle through it, work hard on extra things, and just get back to my old game, and I made it back.

HP: What sorts of things do you work on at practice?

MM: I'm continuously working on all the little skills like face offs. I get my team mates or coaches helping me to work on one-timers. I feel that you have to be able to shoot from any position, even if it's an awkward position because you never know when you get that chance in a game with the puck. It's a skill you have to work on.

HP: What do you think your strengths are on the ice?

MM: Some of my strengths on the ice are my skating; I'm a great skater. I have soft hands, I have a good hockey sense, and I feel that I'm also a very versatile player; I can play the finesse game or the physical shut-down game as well.

HP: How about your weaknesses?

MM: Things I need to improve on, well I always take the attitude that I need to continuously improve in all areas of my game, and I'm confident in working hard to achieve improvement in all areas.

HP: What aspects of your game do you think you really improved on since you started your WHL career?

MM: I see that my skating's gotten a lot faster. My positional-sound game has also developed for me, just game positioning and being smart wherever you are. Whether it's defending the puck or man-on-man coverage, [positioning] has been huge for me.

HP: What's your biggest hockey accomplishment so far?

MM: I think making the Prince Albert Raiders last year was a big accomplishment for me; it was a bit overwhelming, and I was pretty excited to make the team. I also think that getting a letter to the U18 camp this summer has been a pretty big moment for me.

HP: What sorts of things motivate you?

MM: When you play hockey, you have to love the game to play it, so hockey's a sport I love and you don't need too much motivation when you love the game that much.

HP: What is your diet like? Is how and what you eat something that has become important to your career?

MM: Yeah, I eat pretty well, I have a pretty strict diet; I don't eat a lot of carbohydrates. I think I'm at a pretty good weight now with my size. I just eat lean meats, a lot of vegetables, and the odd fruit here or there to stay healthy.

HP: Who are some of the toughest defensemen to beat on 1 on 1 rushes?

MM: I think that going down against Travis Hamonic or Colten Teubert was pretty hard this year. They're two almost NHL-rated defensemen and they're good.

HP: How about some of the toughest defensemen in front of the net? Guys who really make you pay for standing in front of the net.

MM: I'd have to say Colten Teubert again.

HP: Now it's time for our crazy combine question. How much would you charge to wash all the windows at Mario Lemieux's house?

MM: [laughs] I'd probably do it for free. He's one of the greatest to ever play the game. Even to get near him would be special, but to wash his windows would be pretty cool.

# Travis Ewanyk
## LW – Edmonton Oil Kings

Edmonton Oil Kings forward Travis Ewanyk quietly flew under the radar during his first Western Hockey League season.

The 17-year-old from St. Albert certainly didn't have a breakout rookie campaign. In 42 games with the Oil Kings he scored one goal and added four assists, but he showed a lot of promise in his rookie season in particular with the defensive side of his game.

While the Oil Kings struggled to a 16-win season, Ewanyk was one of the bright spots as he was named to Team Pacific for the World U-17 Hockey Challenge in Timmons, Ontario.

This year, Ewanyk is expected to take on a larger role with the Oil Kings, who look to take a step forward from a year ago.

# The Interview

HP: Well Travis, you're heading into your second WHL season, and one thing that's evident in your play is you're a lot more confident.

TE: That one year makes a big difference. Get that one-year under your belt and getting bigger and stronger gives me much more confidence.

HP: Last year under Oil Kings head coach Steve Pleau he would put you out in a lot of defensive situations, and you were able to refine that part of your game. This year we're seeing the confidence when you have the puck on your stick. Are we going to see a more offensive player out of you this year?

TE: That was an area of my game I worked on all summer. I want to be a strong two-way player moving forward. Last year, I really wanted to learn the defensive side of the game at this level. I'm feeling a lot more confident with the puck, and it's something now I need to move forward with.

HP: Last year you got the chance to play for Team Pacific at the World U-17 Hockey Challenge, how did that experience help you heading into the second half of the season?

TE: It gave me confidence knowing that I could play with the elite players of my age group. Being named to the team was a little unexpected, so when I got the chance, I wanted to show that I could play at that level. I didn't want to let that opportunity slip.

HP: What are you looking to improve on most this year?

TE: Consistency. As a 16-year-old, playing the WHL can be a real learning experience and you're bound to make mistakes. This year, I want to be a guy that can be counted on every game and be a guy that can play in all situations.

HP: You have a physical side of your game that many people may not know about. Is that something that has always been part of your game?

TE: I've always been a bit of a gritty player, but I think that it will come out more in junior because you have to use your body. I enjoy the physical side, and I think it's the type of role that I like to play. I think it's a good intangible to have.

HP: How is the new coaching staff with head coach Derek Laxdal and assistant coach Steve Hamilton behind the bench? Are you seeing a different side to these coaches?

TE: You can tell they have a background in winning, and they have a lot of great systems in place and a lot of key fundamentals. It's still training camp, but they demand a lot out of us, and they have high expectations. I really like the change.

HP: Who do you see yourself playing with at this point?

TE: I'm not sure really. They've jumbled the lines up quite a bit so far through training camp, but I'm not really focusing on that. Whoever they decide to play me with this year, I want to be able to build as much chemistry as I can, and be a contributor.

HP: When you think of this being your draft year, do you feel any more added pressure than you have in any other year of your hockey career?

TE: It's certainly in the back of everyone's mind but I'm trying not to think about it. I'd be lying if I said I don't think about, but at the same time, you can't dwell on it, because that can just add more unneeded pressure.

HP: Who's a player that you both look up to and relate to?

TE: A guy like Mike Richards is a role model for me. He brings a lot of skill, but he's got a real mean streak, he plays physical, and because he's a true leader.

HP: Any goals off the ice?

TE: I want to be a leader off the ice, even though I'm a younger guy. I want to be a guy that my teammates can come to in any situation.

HP: When the Oil Kings drafted you, both Bob Green and Randy Hansch viewed you as a future captain. Is that something that has always been in you? Or was it something that you've had to learn over your hockey career?

TE: Every team I played on growing up, I was always the captain. Naturally I find myself being a guy that likes to lead both on the ice and vocally. It would be nice down the road if I was given that honor, but whether I wear a letter on my jersey or not, I'm going to be a leader on this team.

HP: Is there a part of your game that you feel you're underrated in?

TE: I think sometimes I'm not seen as an offensive guy, but I've worked on it hard this summer, and I want that to be something that's tagged onto my game. I know I can be a guy that can chip in offensively and I also can be counted on in all situations.

# Franky Palazzese
## Goalie – Kingston Frontenacs

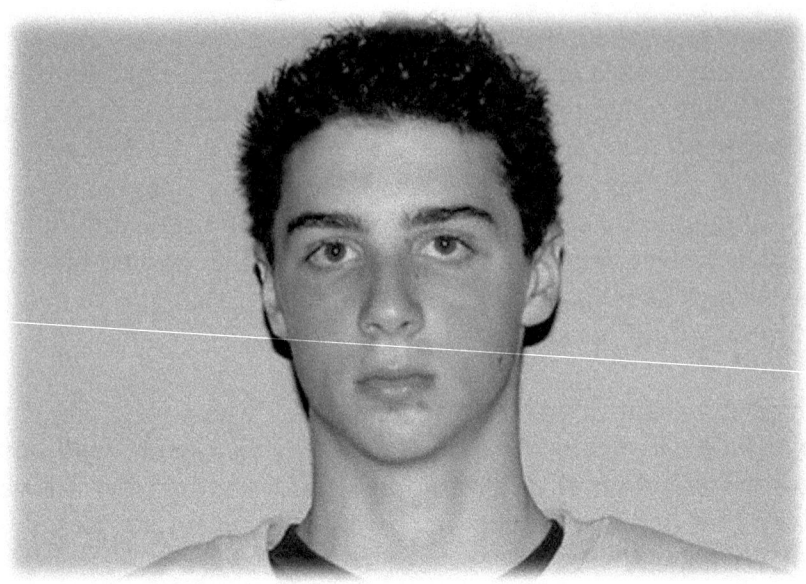

Frank Palazzese was a 4th round selection of the Kingston Frontenacs in the 2009 OHL Priority selection. Palazzese made the Junior A Markham Waxers last season and worked his way up from back-up to playing 8 playoff games where he went 4-4. Palazzese played 29 regular season games posting 16 wins, a 2.81 GAA, 2 shutouts and a .905 save percentage. In the playoffs Franky posted a whopping .931 save percentage and another shutout.

We were high on Palazzese coming out of minor midget and he did nothing last year to change our thinking. Franky is very quick, plays big in the net and has great reaction skills. We think he will really show what he can do once he gets stronger and gets his feet wet in the OHL. We expect Palazzese to push starting tender Philipp Grubauer and perform well in his backup position.

# The Interview

HP: How did your year in Markham go?

FP: It went real well, I thought, last year. I started in as the backup but slowly worked my way into the starting goalie. The team in front of me started to play real well without me, but either way throughout the year, I thought I developed a lot and will be able to go this year.

HP: What was the biggest difference between your 2 games in the OHL and your experience in Markham?

FP: The biggest difference, mainly because I didn't get in any practices, were the shot speeds. I thought sometimes I was a little bit off. Also, the game speed; everyone is stronger and bigger. The first game was tough, but I think with the second game and getting practices in and stuff, I will be fine.

HP: Were those two games enough of a sample size to help you in terms of your development?

FP: Well I think this summer for me was real big. I worked out every day and was on the ice almost every day so the development this summer with my goalie instructor was huge. Those two games really helped me; they gave me a little experience. In the playoffs they brought me up for a week and I got the feel of how it works down there and I got to practice with them. That helped me a lot in terms of working me into the system.

HP: What was your playoff experience like?

FP: It was great. I lived with the goalie, Tyler Beskorowany, and he was great. He taught me everything while I was there, in terms of getting to practice early enough and preparing mentally for games. He showed me the ropes on everything. It was huge because I got that week of practice and living the lifestyle of an OHL player. I think that is important with this being my draft year.

HP: Did you feel like a professional when you were with Kingston?

FP: Mainly you have to act like a professional because that is what they expect of you. But, they also make you feel like a professional. Everywhere you go you are recognized and it makes you feel really good. So, you need to show up when you step on the ice.

HP: What are some of your strengths on the ice?

FP: I think my reaction time is pretty quick so I can adjust to the shot. I can battle to find pucks. Playing the puck has improved for me. I also think my angles are my strongest aspect of my game.

HP: Have you been thinking at all about the NHL draft?

FP: I think it's a little too early but obviously it's something that has been on my mind. That has been my dream since I was a kid. So, now I have a big shot to live my dream so I don't want to let the opportunity go. That's why I work hard every day to make the dream possible. That is what I am working for this year.

HP: Do you have any NHL or OHL goalies you like to model your game after?

FP: In the OHL, Tyler Beskorowany was a huge help for my development. In the NHL, I like to model game after Carey Price. He is so technically sound just like I was taught by my goalie instructor.

HP: What has been the most memorable moment of your hockey career?

FP: Definitely when I got drafted by Kingston In the 4th round in 2009. Waiting there for so long waiting for my name to get called and then to get picked by a great organization like Kingston was a great moment.

# Ryan Nugent-Hopkins
## Center – Red Deer Rebels

Ryan is a Burnaby B.C native who was the 1st overall selection in the 2008 WHL draft by the Rebels. He entered his rookie year with plenty of expectations and he has delivered. In 67 games with Red Deer of the Western Hockey League last season, he netted 24 goals and 41 assists and won Rookie of the Year honors. He also scored the game-winning goal at the 2010 Ivan Hlinka Tournament to beat the United States 1-0 in the championship game. Nugent-Hopkins will almost certainly be a top-five pick with a chance to go first overall.

The truly dominant players shine brightest when the spotlight is on. Not many players have a closer mentality, but even at his young age, Ryan Nugent-Hopkins is one of the few. With his play at the Ivan Hlinka Memorial Tournament and NHL R&D camp, Nugent-Hopkins has only added fuel to his popularity that has spread like wildfire since the beginning of the year. At

6-feet and 160 pounds, he is extremely slight but makes up for it with determination, skill and a solid work ethic.

## The Interview

HP: How did you get started with hockey?

RNH: I started skating when I was about two, and I just really liked it. I started actually playing when I was about four and sort of followed in my brother's footsteps. I basically got into it that way.

HP: How does it feel to play for Red Deer in the Western Hockey League alongside NHL Draft picks?

RNH: It's pretty cool obviously. It's great to play alongside such great players and the experience is invaluable.

HP: What challenges did you face in adjusting to the WHL? What transitions have you undergone to adapt to the style of play and maybe a new role on the team from previous years?

RNH: It's been a big transition. The intensity is a lot higher and everything is so much faster. Even the size of the players is a really big difference.

HP: How has the training regimen differed from lower levels?

RNH: It's quite different. We are on the ice all the time and in the gym after practice. It's a lot tougher, but obviously at this level, more is expected of you.

HP: What do you bring to the table on and off the ice?

RNH: Well, on the ice I try to bring speed and offensive skill and touch. Off the ice I try to be a leader and just do the right things.

HP: Who do you model your game after?

RNH: Not really any one player in particular, but Sidney Crosby is a pretty good example for all of the young kids.

HP: Who were your role-models growing up?

RNH: Joe Sakic is from Burnaby (British Columbia) where I'm from, so I kind of looked up to him. Other players like Joe Thornton and Paul Kariya are guys that I looked up to.

HP: What are your weaknesses? What things do you need to do to take your game to the next level?

RNH: Definitely becoming stronger is something that I need to do. I'm pretty small now, but I have been working hard to improve my strength. I think my shot power could improve too.

HP: What do you think of the competition level in the WHL?

RNH: I think playing in the playoffs against Saskatoon was definitely a challenge. It was a great experience for me because playoff hockey is so different from the regular season, so it was super competitive.

HP: What has been the most memorable moment of your playing career?

RNH: Probably the (Ivan) Hlinka goal. It was just so exciting to be in that situation. It was really cool.

HP: What are your goals for the upcoming season?

RNH: I'd like to go as far in the playoffs as we can. Improving my all-around game is important too, so just improving to go to the next level basically.

HP: How do you think the WHL has helped your development as a player? What do you think of all the traveling involved?

RNH: Quite a lot really. Playing with such high-end guys has really helped my game. The travel is pretty difficult really, but it gets taken care of pretty well. It's overwhelming at first, but you get used to it.

HP: Some say the WHL has a reputation as a physical league with maybe not as much offensive talent as the QMJHL or OHL. Is that a fair assessment?

RNH: Well I think we are more physical, but there are definitely a lot of skilled players in the league too. I think that's maybe a misconception because there are a lot of really talented players in the WHL.

HP: What do you think of the rivalry between the United States and Canada? Russia-Canada used to be the big rivalry. Why do you think the U.S. has been so successful of late?

RNH: I think it's great. I think they've been developing a lot of great players. There are obviously more kids playing hockey, and they've done a really good job of developing those players to compete at a high level. With more kids interested, it's going to make the teams better. They really have been improving a lot.

HP: How does it feel to be rated as a potential first-round pick in the NHL Draft?

RNH: It's pretty cool. It's surreal really. You dream about that kind of thing and for it to be reality is unreal.

HP: Have any already-drafted players given you any advice?

RNH: Yeah, for sure. The guys tell me to just kind of play my game and not worry about it. It will take care of itself if I just go out there and do what I can do.

HP: If you could make a pitch to an NHL team on why they should draft you, what would you say?

RNH: I'd tell them that I can bring a constant, hard work ethic. I'd try to work as hard as I can every day. I think I have some good offensive skill, and I'm working on my two-way game. I definitely will try to be a leader too.

# Reece Scarlett
## Defense – Swift Current Broncos

Reece Scarlett is quietly making a name for himself amongst National Hockey League scouts. The smooth skating defenseman played a big role as a 16-year-old with the Swift Current Broncos. The early season trade of veteran defenseman Eric Doyle pushed a lot of responsibility on to the Sherwood Park, Alberta native.

He played in 65 games scoring one goal and 10 points, while adding 49 penalty minutes. The Broncos were swept in the first round of the WHL playoffs by the Memorial Cup finalist, Brandon Wheat Kings. In four games, Scarlett tallied two assists.

Scarlett also represented Team Pacific at the World U-17 Hockey Challenge last year, and was invited to Canada's U-18 camp for the Ivan Hlinka tournament this summer.
Scarlett won a Western Canadian Bantam AAA championship with the Sherwood Park Flyers in 2008.

The 17-year-old is looking to be one of the leaders on the blueline for the Broncos this upcoming season.

## The Interview

HP: Can you describe your rookie season in the Western Hockey League?

RS: It was everything I wanted it to be and more. We had a real good team, and I was fortunate enough to be in a situation where I was able to play more than what a lot of 16-year-old's are able to.

HP: Growing up just outside of Edmonton, your parents are billets to the Edmonton Oil Kings players? Can you talk about what that experience was like and who you billeted?

RS: We had Robin Figren, a (third round) draft pick of the New York Islanders who is from Sweden. He's a great guy. I still keep in touch with him today. He showed me how much fun he had playing in the league. There was no question after he lived with us, that I would be going the route. He's a huge influence in my life. I have his jersey in my room here in Swift Current. He taught me how to enjoy hockey for what it is. He means a lot in my life. He's like a brother to me.

HP: Now that you're in the WHL playing with Swift Current, and your parents are still billeting for the Oil Kings, does it feel a little strange for you?

RS: It's almost like a funny co-incidence. I know the guys that are living in the house. I became best friends with Travis Ewanyk, who lived in our house last year. I've played with and against him since I was seven.

HP: Former NHL'er Mark Lamb was in his first season behind the bench of the Swift Current Broncos. How was he to play for in your rookie season?

RS: He's a great guy, he played in the NHL for a long time. He knows what it takes to make an impact in the NHL. Overall, he taught me how to handle myself and carry myself as a player both on and off the ice. He has also showed me how important the little tidbits of information can be. My ears are always open, and anything he tells me I take in and use it the best way I can.

HP: You play in Swift Current, the smallest market in the Western Hockey League. How is it playing in such a small market?

RS: I didn't know what to expect at the beginning. Everybody mentions it's a small market. People know you, people love you. That's all you can ask for in a city is people supporting you. There is so much history with this team. We have a great group of core guys that can do nothing but work hard for the fans.

HP: The Swift Current Broncos have a rich tradition in the WHL, and have a strong record in moving players on to the professional ranks. What's it like to play for the same organization as a future hall of famer Joe Sakic?

RS: There is a rich history. We have pictures of everybody who played in the NHL, and just seeing their pictures every day makes you strive to be just like them, and you never forget it. Hopefully this year for myself, and guys like Adam Lowry and Graeme Craige we all can get drafted and one day, carry on the tradition.

HP: Last year you got a chance to represent Team Pacific at the World U-17 Hockey Challenge in Timmons, Ontario as well as play in the playoffs with Swift Current. This year you are looking towards the 2011 draft. It's been a very busy two years. How do you reflect on the past two years?

RS: Getting drafted into the WHL, you still don't realize the level of hockey it is, and the opportunity you have playing in this league. Seeing guys last year that you played against in Midget that are getting drafted in the NHL, it makes you realize just how quick everything approaches.

HP: You played 65 games in the regular season on the blueline as a 16-year-old and you one goal and 10 points. What are your expectations heading into this year and what are your biggest strengths?

RS: Throughout my career, I've been a great skater and I try to view myself as a first pass kind of defenceman. I feel I've got good hockey sense in reading the defensive end and reading the play.
There certainly is pressure to succeed in your draft year, but more than anything it's still just a hockey season. Ultimately I'm trying to win a championship with Swift Currrent, and if we can have a good season, good things will come out of it for me.

HP: What are some of the key areas of the game you need to focus on?

RS: I have always been told to get a little more physical and finish my checks.

HP: Growing up just outside of Edmonton you played the majority of your games in midget and bantam around the Edmonton area. How were you able to adjust to the long road trips in the WHL?

RS: It's tough to change from a good 20 minute drive with your parents to six hour bus rides. Learn to sleep and do homework on the bus. It took awhile to adjust, but I just tried to relax and talk with the guys, and once I got bored, I would just throw my iPod on and just stare out the window and try to get some sleep.

HP: Who are some of your teammates that you've tried to learn and model your game around?

RS: Last year (defenceman) Derek Claffey, our captain and my defence partner, was a big influence on me. I sat beside him in the room. He's a good character guy to learn from, and I just tried to pick his brain as much as I could. This year, to see and learn from a player like Cody Eakin, you can't help but learn from a guy like him. He knows where he wants to go, and he's always working hard, and he's the perfect role model.

HP: Is there a player that you played with or against growing up that has been through the NHL draft that you've been able to learn from?

RS: Mark Pysyk (2010 Buffalo Sabres first round pick) is from the same city as I am. I've never actually played with him, but I've known him almost my whole life. He's always been a poised defenceman. He's a great character guy, and you can learn a lot from watching him.

HP: You certainly be honored to have any team draft you come June, but if there was one team you'd want to be drafted by, who would it be?

RS: Growing up in Edmonton, I took a lot of heat with my favorite team being the Calgary Flames, but I still would have to say the Flames.

HP: Your head coach Mark Lamb is a former Edmonton Oiler. Does he know that you're a Flames fan?

RS: Not sure if he knows that or not, but hopefully he doesn't get too offended by it.

HP: You've had some discussions with some NHL scouts, and they're apt to throw a curveball question at you from time to time. Have they given you any weird questions to answer?

RS: Not yet, they've all been pretty basic questions, but I've heard the rumors. We'll see how it goes when I get to that point.

HP: Well since you haven't got any strange questions from NHL scouts yet, we'll give you one to prepare yourself for when they come flying your way. How many marbles can you fit inside of a mini-van?

RS: A mini-van? Wow, a lot. I guess it depends how big the mini-van is.

Note:

We attempted to contact an additional 25+ players to include in this book. Reasons for some players not being included ranged from teams not getting back to us, player agents deciding not to allow interviews and a few Euros not confident enough in their command of the English language.

We tried to include a wide range of players. We have high end first round prospects and other prospects who could turn out to be "on the bubble" next June.

As the season moves along we will continue to provide interviews on our website and always provide information on prospects through game reports and full player scouting reports.

Our 2011 NHL Draft Guide will be released in May 2011.

Another NHL Draft season is about to begin and we have already been all over the rinks scouting events such as the NHL Rookie camps, CHL pre-season games and 2011 OHL, WHL and QMJHL draft prospects.

I'm looking forward to taking a season long look at the prospects for the 2011 NHL Draft. I have seen some players many times already and other players limited times.

I'm not a big fan of pre-season ranking lists. I just think that it is more of a fan thing than anything else. To rank players we have seen over 50 times against players we have seen minimal times makes little sense to me.

Our QMJHL scouts are already off and running as the QMJHL season started a week ago. I have already setup my own travel plans to scout that league throughout the season.

I'm looking forward to watching a few players that I expect to make a name for themselves this season. I think of players like Zach Bell in Brampton who might fly up the rankings if he brings the physical game he can play on a more regular basis.. I'll be watching Travis Ewanyk and Klarc Wilson to jump a bit more into the mainstream draft spotlight, both are fantastic players who are getting even better in a hurry. I'll be expecting Andrew D'Agostini to steal the starting goalie job in Peterborough. He is 5'10" so he, like JP Anderson before him, will be NHL Draft challenged. If D'Agostini can grow an inch or two this year, lookout, because this kid can really stop pucks. There are many other players we feel are under the radar right now. Keep visiting HockeyProspect.com to stay on top of them.

It's a fun time of year so sit back and enjoy!

Mark Edwards,
HockeyProspect.com Founder

# Acknowledgements

A big thanks to the following for helping to make this pre-season NHL Prospects book come together.

Alex Linsky
Andrew Echevarria
Jason Hills
Simon Larouche
Steve Fitzsimmons
Cameron Rudolph
Ron Berman

The OHL, WHL and QMJHL teams
The UHSL
The NHL

All the photographers whose fantastic photos are used both in this book and on our website.

"Three Horse Race" by Cameron Rudolph

## Scouting Staff

Rob Basso

Dave Toledano

Ron Berman

Alex Linsky

Jason Hills

Bruno Simard

Dan Rogers

Mark Edwards

Simon Larouche

Justin Schreiber

Ryan Yessie

## Writers

Cameron Rudolph

Steve Fitzsimmons

## Founder

Mark Edwards

www.ingramcontent.com/pod-product-compliance
Lightning Source LLC
Chambersburg PA
CBHW071459040426
42444CB00008B/1407